Beginner's Guide to Instructional Design

*Identify and Examine Learning Needs,
Knowledge Delivery Methods, and
Approaches to Design Learning Material*

Purnima Valiathan

www.bpbonline.com

Copyright © 2022 BPB Online

All rights reserved. No part of this book may be reproduced, stored in a retrieval system, or transmitted in any form or by any means, without the prior written permission of the publisher, except in the case of brief quotations embedded in critical articles or reviews.

Every effort has been made in the preparation of this book to ensure the accuracy of the information presented. However, the information contained in this book is sold without warranty, either express or implied. Neither the author, nor BPB Online or its dealers and distributors, will be held liable for any damages caused or alleged to have been caused directly or indirectly by this book.

BPB Online has endeavored to provide trademark information about all of the companies and products mentioned in this book by the appropriate use of capitals. However, BPB Online cannot guarantee the accuracy of this information.

Group Product Manager: Marianne Conor
Publishing Product Manager: Eva Brawn
Senior Editor: Connell
Content Development Editor: Melissa Monroe
Technical Editor: Anne Stokes
Copy Editor: Joe Austin
Language Support Editor: Justin Baldwin
Project Coordinator: Tyler Horan
Proofreader: Khloe Styles
Indexer: V. Krishnamurthy
Production Designer: Malcolm D'Souza
Marketing Coordinator: Kristen Kramer

First published: March 2022

Published by BPB Online
WeWork, 119 Marylebone Road
London NW1 5PU

UK | UAE | INDIA | SINGAPORE

ISBN 978-93-55510-778

www.bpbonline.com

Dedicated to

My beloved Parents:

K. Sethumadhavan
Uma Sethumadhavan

About the Author

Purnima Valiathan holds a Bachelor's degree in Education and has over 25 years of teaching and training experience. As a teacher, she has experience in physical classroom teaching and virtual teaching. As an instructional designer, Purnima has worked on various projects that involved the application of instructional design, technology, and media to address the learning needs of both the student learner and the adult learner. She has written a number of papers and articles, which have been published/presented in prestigious forums, such as International Society for Performance Improvement (ISPI), American Society of Training and Development (ASTD, now ATD), and Training Journal, a magazine published in the United Kingdom. Currently, she runs an instructional design training and consultancy firm, which provides instructional design training to teachers, trainers, and instructional designers in classroom and online mode through the portal, **www.purnima-valiathan.com**.

About the Reviewer

Sarbani Bose has a Master's degree in English Literature. She joined the domain of instructional design about 26 years ago. What fascinated her the most over the years was 'why' and 'how' adults learn. Her work-related travels to different nations, and the opportunity she received while observing the various kinds of learners there, helped her to be open to all kinds of possibilities while creating the learning solutions. Analyzing the learner profiles, performing needs and gap analysis, and designing customized learning solutions based on instructional theories, frameworks, models, and common sense, have been her area of expertise. She has worked with reputed organizations in the education domain such as NIIT, Lionbridge, and Tech Mahindra, creating content for their diverse customer base. The verticals that she has worked on are IT (Hardware and Software), Manufacturing, Telecom, Soft Skills, Aviation, Management Skills, Multiple Intelligences, Ergonomics, Health, and Insurance, and K12. Sarbani believes that learner centric training is the key to closing the knowledge gaps and enhancing the performance at workplace or in any other domain.

Acknowledgement

There are a few people I want to thank for their continued support during the writing of this book. First and foremost, I would like to thank my parents for instilling in me the thirst for knowledge, which turned me into a lifelong learner and gave me the courage to pursue different career paths. I am also very grateful to my husband and son for their constant support, without which this book would not have been written.

I am thankful to my alma mater Central Institute of Education, Delhi University, which first introduced me to educational psychology, a subject that soon became my passion. I am extremely appreciative of Mr. Neeraj Agarwal, who recruited me as an Instructional Designer at NIIT, paving the way for me to hone my skills in this profession. I am also indebted to Sarbani Bose, my former colleague and an expert in instructional design, for reviewing my book from a technical standpoint. I also want to thank my friend, Naveen Nischal for helping me with the images and graphics included in this book.

Last, but not the least, I extend my gratitude to the team at BPB Publications for being there to support and encourage me, and allowing me to extend the deadline when professional commitments came in the way of my writing the book. Without their support, I wouldn't have been able to share my knowledge and experience with the instructional design community.

Preface

Instructional design is a vast and evolving field that is influenced by various disciplines, such as education, psychology, training, technology, and media. The problem with attempting to write a book on this subject is that it is impossible to address everything without running the risk of making it heavy in theory. Therefore, the attempt in this book is to seamlessly merge theory and practice.

- The theory of instructional design: Instructional design or ID can be defined from different perspectives – as a process, as a system, and as a discipline or field. From a process perspective, ID is a set of activities, which are undertaken for designing instruction with the goal of optimising learning experiences to achieve specific objectives. From a discipline perspective, it is a branch of knowledge concerned with translating general principles of learning and instruction into plans for instructional materials and learning. From a systems perspective, it is an arrangement of policies, resources, and procedures to promote learning and achieve performance and business goals. This book focuses primarily on the process and discipline aspects.

- The practice of instructional design: ADDIE is a systematic and sequential approach to instructional design. It is also a popular model adopted by most instructional designers. There are other models too that have emerged over the years, but are not significantly different from ADDIE. In this book, the ADDIE methodology is addressed because it is simple, effective, and has a wider applicability with modified versions available for K-12 and Higher Education. In fact, the entire book is structured around this model, with each chapter focusing on one of the phases in this model. In addition, instructional design is applicable in all areas dealing with any kind of learning – K-12, higher education, corporate training, and vocational skills training. Therefore, in this book, we will address the application of the ADDIE model and ID principles across all these domains.

Chapter 1 will describe instructional design and its significance in designing instructional material. Various ID models will be covered with specific focus on ADDIE and the Dick & Carey model. The chapter will also address the variables and constants that influence instructional design. Finally, the chapter will compare the instructional design process with Design Thinking, which has become popular in both educational institutions and corporate organizations.

Chapter 2 will address the Analysis phase in the ADDIE model in detail. The chapter will cover the variables to be considered in this phase. It will also explain how this phase is completed in K-12, higher education, vocational skills, and corporate training.

Chapter 3 will cover the Design phase of the ADDIE model with the focus on content organizing and structuring. It will address how the strengths and limitations of the human brain and memory must be considered when creating the course and program outlines.

Chapter 4 will continue with the Design phase and introduce the concept of learning outcomes and their significance in the design of instructional materials. Further, it will cover the different types of learning outcomes, and how these manifest across K-12, higher education, vocational skills, and corporate training.

Chapter 5 will cover instructional design at a macro-level, again a part of the Design phase in the ADDIE model. This chapter will address the behaviorist, cognitive, and constructivist schools of learning. It will also present some frameworks that map to these schools, such as Direct Instruction, Gagne's Events of Instruction, Kolb's Experiential Model, and Merrill's principles. These frameworks will be explained and illustrated using examples from K-12, higher education, vocational skills, and corporate training.

Chapter 6 will address instructional design at the micro-level, which is the Development phase in the ADDIE model. It will explain how the information that is to be learned should be presented using Ruth Clark's framework for information mapping. This chapter will also address how different strategies can be used to elucidate different types of content, and the ancillary material that can be developed to support vocational and corporate training needs.

Chapter 7 will delve into the Implement phase, and address the concepts of synchronous and asynchronous online learning, blended learning, and flipped classroom in K-12. It will also provide an explanation of the various technologies that are used to facilitate online learning, such as learning management systems, collaboration software, learning experience platforms, and authoring tools.

Chapter 8 will address the Evaluation phase of the ADDIE model. It will cover the various terms associated with evaluation, such as quiz, test, and formative and summative assessments. In addition, it will present different strategies for assessing the learners and assessment tools, such as rubrics, checklists, and rating scales for assessing specific learning outcomes.

Chapter 9 will present four case studies depicting how instructional design was applied to meet specific learning outcomes – one from each domain – K-12, higher education, vocational skills, and professional training.

Coloured Images

Please follow the link to download the *Coloured Images* of the book:

https://rebrand.ly/765a41

We have code bundles from our rich catalogue of books and videos available at **https://github.com/bpbpublications**. Check them out!

Errata

We take immense pride in our work at BPB Publications and follow best practices to ensure the accuracy of our content to provide with an indulging reading experience to our subscribers. Our readers are our mirrors, and we use their inputs to reflect and improve upon human errors, if any, that may have occurred during the publishing processes involved. To let us maintain the quality and help us reach out to any readers who might be having difficulties due to any unforeseen errors, please write to us at :

errata@bpbonline.com

Your support, suggestions and feedbacks are highly appreciated by the BPB Publications' Family.

Did you know that BPB offers eBook versions of every book published, with PDF and ePub files available? You can upgrade to the eBook version at www.bpbonline.com and as a print book customer, you are entitled to a discount on the eBook copy. Get in touch with us at :

business@bpbonline.com for more details.

At **www.bpbonline.com**, you can also read a collection of free technical articles, sign up for a range of free newsletters, and receive exclusive discounts and offers on BPB books and eBooks.

Piracy

If you come across any illegal copies of our works in any form on the internet, we would be grateful if you would provide us with the location address or website name. Please contact us at **business@bpbonline.com** with a link to the material.

If you are interested in becoming an author

If there is a topic that you have expertise in, and you are interested in either writing or contributing to a book, please visit **www.bpbonline.com**. We have worked with thousands of developers and tech professionals, just like you, to help them share their insights with the global tech community. You can make a general application, apply for a specific hot topic that we are recruiting an author for, or submit your own idea.

Reviews

Please leave a review. Once you have read and used this book, why not leave a review on the site that you purchased it from? Potential readers can then see and use your unbiased opinion to make purchase decisions. We at BPB can understand what you think about our products, and our authors can see your feedback on their book. Thank you!

For more information about BPB, please visit **www.bpbonline.com**.

Table of Contents

1. **Understanding Instructional Design** 1
   - Introduction 1
   - Structure 2
   - Objectives 2
   - Decoding instructional design 2
   - Instructional design definitions 2
     - *Variables and constants in instructional design* 3
     - *Is instructional design science or art?* 4
   - Significance of instructional design 5
     - *Evolution of technology* 5
     - *Need for collaboration* 6
   - Instructional design models 7
     - *Instructional systems design* 8
     - *Dick and Carey model* 8
     - *ADDIE model* 10
     - *ADDIE and Dick & Carey model–a Comparison* 14
     - *Other models* 14
   - Instructional design versus design thinking 15
   - Conclusion 16
   - Points to remember 16
   - Multiple choice questions 17
     - *Answers* 18
   - Questions 18
   - Key terms 18

2. **Analyzing Learning Need** 19
   - Introduction 19
   - Structure 20
   - Objectives 20

Significance of analysis 20
Analysis for workplace skills 22
    Understanding an adult learner 23
    Challenges in workplace analysis 25
    Understanding the vocational student 27
Job analysis 29
Analysis in education 32
    Higher education 32
    K-12 34
    Age-related differences 35
    Contextual differences 36
Conclusion 37
Points to remember 37
Multiple choice questions 38
    Answers 39
Questions 39
Key terms 39

3. Designing the Outline 41
Introduction 41
Structure 42
Objectives 42
Memory stages 42
Working memory 44
Cognitive load theory 46
Design implications 50
Patterning 51
Outline design 52
    Workplace learning 52
    Higher education 55
    Vocational skills 56
    Declarative and procedural knowledge 57

  K-12 curriculum 58
 Conclusion 58
 Points to remember 59
 Multiple choice questions 59
  Answers 60
 Questions 60
 Key terms 61

4. Defining Learning Outcomes 63
 Introduction 63
 Structure 64
 Objectives 64
 Different terminologies 64
 Purpose of learning outcomes 66
 Frameworks for learning outcomes 66
  Mager's format 67
  Bloom's taxonomy 68
  Descriptive versus prescriptive frameworks 71
  Critiquing Bloom's taxonomy 71
  A workaround to Bloom's taxonomy 72
  Writing learning outcomes 73
   Outcomes for workplace learning 74
   Outcomes in higher education 75
   Outcomes for vocational training 76
   Outcomes in K-12 77
 Conclusion 79
 Points to remember 79
 Multiple choice questions 80
  Answers 81
 Questions 81
 Key terms 81

5. Designing Instructional Material ... 83
Structure ... 84
Objectives ... 84
Introduction ... 84
Popular learning theories ... 84
- *Behaviorist theory* ... 85
- *Cognitive theory* ... 86
- *Constructivist theory* ... 86
- *Pedagogy* ... 87
- *Andragogy* ... 87
- *Heutagogy* ... 88

Learning frameworks ... 89
- *Direct instruction* ... 89
- *Gagne's events of instruction* ... 90
- *Applying direct instruction and Gagne's events* ... 94
- *Merrill's First principles* ... 94
- *Applying Merrill's framework* ... 95
- *Kolb's Experiential model* ... 95
- *Applying Kolb's model* ... 96
- *Comparing the frameworks* ... 97
- *Picking a learning framework* ... 98

Motivation theories ... 98
- *Intrinsic and extrinsic motivation* ... 98
- *Value-Expectancy theory* ... 99
- *Keller's ARCS model* ... 99
- *Learner engagement and interactivity* ... 100

Conclusion ... 101
Points to remember ... 101
Multiple choice questions ... 102
- *Answers* ... 103

Questions ... 103
Key terms ... 104

6. Developing Instructional Material 105
Structure 106
Objectives 106
Content-types framework 108
Facts 109
Concepts 110
Non-examples 111
Procedures 112
Processes 113
Principles 114
Scenarios 115
Case studies 115
Stories 115
Deciding how to present information 116
Visuals 117
Storyboard 119
Developing storyboards 119
Storyboard format 120
Job aids 122
Conclusion 123
Points to remember 124
Multiple choice questions 125
Answers 125
Questions 126
Key terms 126

7. Delivery Strategies 127
Structure 128
Objectives 128
Teaching-learning process 128
Evolution of online learning 129
Types of online learning 130

  Synchronous learning 130
  Asynchronous learning 131
  Flipped classroom 132
  Blended learning 132
 Online learning technology 132
  Learning management systems 132
  Learning experience platforms 133
 Comparing asynchronous online learning and classroom teaching 134
 Virtual instructor-led teaching 136
  Working of VILT 136
  Collaborating in VILT sessions 137
  Using breakout rooms 137
  Planning for online teaching 138
 Conclusion 139
 Points to remember 140
 Multiple choice questions 140
  Answers 141
 Questions 141
 Key terms 142

8. Assessment Strategies 143
 Structure 144
 Objectives 144
 Understanding evaluation 144
 Types of assessments 145
  Formative and summative assessments 145
  Designing formative assessments 146
   Placement 147
   Challenge 147
   Feedback 147
  Summative assessment/evaluation 147
   Reliability 148

    Validity *148*
    Difficulty index *148*
    Discrimination index *149*
  Assessing declarative knowledge 149
    Multiple choice questions *149*
    Multi-select questions *150*
    Fill in the blank *151*
    Matching questions *151*
    Subjective questions *152*
  Assessing procedural knowledge 152
    Assessment tools *153*
    Rating scales *153*
    Checklists *154*
    Rubrics *155*
    Anecdotal notes *155*
  Evaluating workplace training 155
    Kirkpatrick model *156*
    Challenges in measuring training ROI *156*
  Conclusion 157
  Points to remember 157
  Multiple Choice Questions 158
    Answers *159*
  Questions 159
  Key terms 159

9. Case Studies 161
  Structure 162
  Objectives 162
  Introduction 162
    Engagement versus time/cost *162*
    Effectiveness versus time/cost *163*
    One-time investment versus recurring costs *163*

Case study 1 – Mathematics anxiety 164
    Background 164
    Solution – Adaptive approach 165
    Personal tutoring 166
    Exercise design 167
Case study 2 – Entrepreneurship orientation program 171
    Background 172
    Solution–Task-based approach 173
Case study 3 – Instructional design certification 177
    Background 178
    Solution–Comprehensive Scaffolding Framework (CSF)© 179
    Certification levels 180
Case study 4 – Financial inclusion program 181
    Background 182
    Solution–Story-based approach 182
    Conclusion 184

Index 185-191

CHAPTER 1
Understanding Instructional Design

Introduction

Sometimes you see them, sometimes you don't. They could be the quiet ones, listening intently, holding on to every word that you speak in class, or they could be the ones who speak out so often and so loud that it drowns every other voice around. They could also be the ones, sitting miles away from you, reading what you have written, or listening to what you have to say – trying to learn from the knowledge and experience that you have chosen to share with them.

Or perhaps, they could be the young ones, for whom the mobile is their world – holding everything they possess – identity, friends, wallet, music, movies, and yes, even the learning material.

Who are they? Well, they could be your potential learner. And as you can see, you cannot pigeon-hole them. They could be meek or demanding, active or passive, motivated or bored – but they are there to learn. It is up to you to hold their interest, and help them gain knowledge and develop their skills. It is a tough call, but once you get to know them – with all their queerness and eccentricities, challenges and constraints, brilliance and inquisitiveness – you will understand what works for them and what doesn't. This, in turn, will help you serve them content, "just right".

Instructional design, with its learner-centric approach, helps you achieve this.

Structure

In this chapter, we will discuss the following topics:

- Definition of instructional design
- Significance of instructional design
- Instructional design models
- Instructional design versus design thinking

Objectives

After studying this chapter, you will be able to understand the process of instructional design and appreciate its significance in designing the learning materials. You will also be able to identify the popular instructional design models, and describe the ADDIE model. Finally, you will analyze the similarities and differences between instructional design and design thinking.

Decoding instructional design

Did you ever struggle to learn something as a student, or maybe even as an adult? And, then you found this person, a book, or a video that explained it so elegantly and with such simple logic that you immediately grasped it? Putting it simply, this is what instructional design is. But, a book on instructional design cannot stop at presenting a simple explanation of the concept, right? So, let us move on to the academic definition of this term.

Instructional design definitions

If we consider instructional design as a discipline, then it may be defined as a field of study that is concerned with the application of scientific principles to create instructional plans and materials. Considered as a process, it is a systematic set of activities that you undertake in order to design instructional material.

So, how is instructional design different from teaching or training?

Let's take the example of a typical classroom learning session. There is a teacher or facilitator who uses some material to explain a topic or demonstrate a skill. The teacher may create the instructional material, plan the sequence of instructional events, or even use instructional material designed by somebody else. The instructional material could be a book, a video lesson, or an online multimedia module. When we take such a view, we can identify many entities in the learning process, and teaching appears to be a small, though significant part of it. In the book, *Principles of Instructional Design*, by Gagne, Briggs and Wager, the authors state the following:

"Instruction may include events that are generated by a page of print, by a picture, by a television program, or by a combination of physical objects, among other things. Of course, a teacher may play an essential role in the arrangement of any of these events. Or, as already mentioned, the learners may be able to manage instructional events themselves. Teaching, then, may be considered as only one form of instruction, albeit a signally important one."

Instructional design assumes that learning occurs within a system made up of various entities and components, and instruction is planned, designed, and developed through a systematic process. This view brings us to yet another definition of instructional design – one from a systems perspective. As per this definition, learning is a process that occurs within a system made up of entities such as learners and instructors, and objects, such as curriculum, books, technology and tools.

Table 1.1 provides a summary of the definitions from different perspectives:

Perspective	Definition
Process	Planned set of activities undertaken in a consistent manner to facilitate learning.
Discipline	Field of study which involves the application of scientific principles to create instructional materials.
System	A model with interconnected components for designing, developing, and evaluating instruction.

Table 1.1: Definitions of instructional design

Note: In recent times, there is an increasing trend to refer to instructional design as learning design. In this book, we will be using the traditional term, instructional design.

Variables and constants in instructional design

Why don't you do a quick mental exercise? Go back to your student days, and think of something that you learned – it could be anything – riding a bicycle in the park, learning mathematics in school, or engineering in college. Now think why you learned this – obviously to achieve a goal – to ride the bicycle in the first case, acquire numeracy skills in the second, and get a professional degree that would fetch you a good job, in the third, right?

What we are getting at here is that there are variables in any learning situation, and these are, audience, content, and the learning outcome. For example, as a K-12 student (audience), you learned mathematics (content) in order to understand and apply it in life (outcome). Or, as a graduate student (audience), you enrolled in the engineering course (content) to pursue a career (outcome) as an engineer.

Instructional design teaches us to analyze the context in every learning situation. This context is made up of three variables – the **audience** that is the learner, the **content** to be taught, and the **learning outcome**.

The following is an example of the variables in instructional design:

Example 1.1: Variables in instructional design

Audience: K-12

Content: Mathematics

Outcome: Life skills

The following is another example of the variables in instructional design:

Example 1.2: Variables in instructional design

Audience: Graduate student

Content: Engineering

Outcome: Career skills

Additionally, instructional design as a discipline rests upon some constants – the scientific principles of **memory**, **learning** and **motivation**. These principles influence the design of instructional processes and the creation of instructional material.

Is instructional design science or art?

Science is about experimentation and empirical evidence, while art boasts of creativity. Just like cooking is both science and art, instructional design is too. To get started, you need some essential ingredients, and a few tested recipes. Instructional design models and principles are scientific in nature, while how you design the instructional process depends upon creativity – the art. Once you understand the principles, you can get started with designing the learner-centric material. However, it will bode well to remember that these principles will get you started, but to make instruction effective and engaging, you must infuse it with insights and lots of passion, just like a good chef does. And that my dear reader is the art in instructional design – one which you will master with loads and loads of practice. And if this art ever goes missing from your instructional piece, it will end up as fast food to be picked up in a hurry on the go, just to be had to fill the tummy, and not for nutrition or enjoyment.

As the famous chef, Dylan Jones, says:

"Recipes don't work unless you use your heart."

Well, instructional design models and principles will not work either, unless you infuse the solution with insights and passion.

> **Note:** "Instructional Design is the art and science of creating an instructional environment and materials that will bring the learner from the state of not being able to accomplish certain tasks to the state of being able to accomplish those tasks. Instructional Design is based on theoretical and practical research in the areas of cognition, educational psychology, and problem solving." – Broderick C.L. (2001)

Significance of instructional design

The goal of designing instruction is to help learners learn. This learning can occur in classroom settings, home settings, or virtual settings. The learner could be a school student, a college-going young adult, a distance learner, or a working professional. So, you see, instructional design is applicable regardless of the learner's profile or delivery media. However, there are a couple of factors that has led to its popularity in recent times.

Evolution of technology

Technology is no longer a supplementary tool in the learning process that is used to deliver a few topics here and there. In many situations, it is the primary tool, as is evident from the number of online learning programs, portals, and apps that have become available for the K-12 students, graduate students, and working professionals.

When you see a toddler with a mobile phone, you may think she is playing. But ask the toddler's parents, and they will tell you that the mobile phone is their toddler's first encounter with learning – except that it is not within a bricks and mortar one. When a middle-school student surfs the YouTube channel, you cannot assume that it is for recreation, for he could be trying to gain clarity on a concept that he didn't quite grasp in school. These situations indicate how the learning ecosystem is undergoing a change, and is becoming more and more demand based. Learners today have a lot of choices since technology has made information accessible anytime, anywhere. As K-12, higher education, and corporate learning increasingly move towards being multi-modal and technology-driven, instructional design assumes an even greater significance. If we want to engage our learners, our learning material must be learner-centric, and instructional design helps us in achieving that.

Need for collaboration

A good learning experience requires the instructional process and the instructional material to be effective both in content and pedagogy. It is rare to find a single person with a deep understanding of both the areas. With the proliferation of technology, an understanding of tools and media has also become necessary.

Content experts are well-versed with the content to be disseminated (the "what" of learning), but may not be as knowledgeable with the methodology (the "how" of learning). This can make the material that they design content-centric. On the other hand, the instructional design process begins with understanding the learner, thereby making the material learner-centric. This difference is captured in *Figure 1.1*:

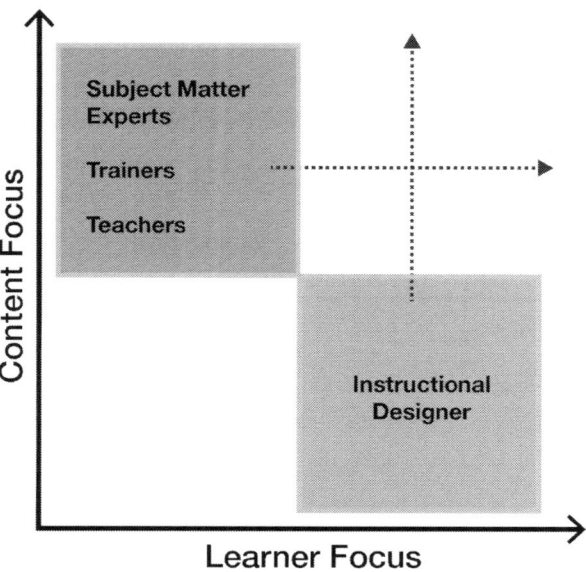

Figure 1.1: Content versus Learner Focus

Given the hectic schedules that the content experts follow, they may not always know how to teach online, or which tools to use. This may result in them uploading the presentation slides or video lectures as online learning. Integrating **information communication technology** (**ICT**) with content in the best possible way is yet another challenge they face.

Finally, the online learner is not under direct supervision of the teacher, therefore the engagement component becomes crucial in this medium. Content experts may know how to engage students in class, but when it comes to online delivery, they may not use the right strategy to engage the learner. Even if the class is being conducted in a physical classroom, at times, they may require using technology and media to present certain concepts, especially the abstract ones, in an engaging way.

Instructional design adopts a planned and systematic approach to the design of instructional material, and instructional designers understand the learning theories, instructional frameworks, and engagement strategies. Hence, collaboration between content experts and instructional designers can help create effective instructional material. *Table 1.2* depicts the competencies of each role:

Content expert competencies	Instructional designer competencies
Subject matter	Learning theories
Examples and non-examples	Instructional frameworks
Learner misconceptions	Technology and media tools
	Ideal delivery medium

Table 1.2: Content expert and instructional designer competencies

Here is an analogy to further illustrate this point. Think of any favorite movie of yours. When you were watching the movie, you would have rarely thought about all the behind-the-scenes action that went into creating the movie. But the fact is that movie-making is a collaboration between people with a diverse set of skills. Script-writers, directors, music directors, set designers, and actors – all come together to create magic on screen. This is a collaborative activity and cannot be achieved by a single person. Instructional material too is designed by experts from diverse fields – content, teaching, media, and technology.

The future of instruction is beautifully captured in the following quote by Professor Woodie Flowers, from the department of Engineering Design at MIT:

"In their highly developed form, learning materials would be as elegantly produced as movies and video games, and would be as engaging as a great novel."

Instructional design models

When you started cooking, you may have referred to recipes often. You may adopt this approach for a while, until such time that you master a few dishes. Over time, you will be able to cook a fairly decent meal without referring to recipes. However, if you want to try out a new dish, then you will refer to a recipe. There is nothing very novel about this, as most of us follow a similar approach – using some form of guidance and support when we learn a new task, and as we gain expertise, complete the task automatically. Instructional design models can be considered as recipes for designing instructional interventions. It provides novice instructional designers with a framework to follow in the initial stages of their career. One more advantage of adopting these models is that it helps you to always keep your focus on the learner.

Instructional systems design

A key tenet of instructional design is that learning occurs within a system. The examples are the *educational system* for K-12, the *university system* for higher education, and the *training systems* in corporate organizations. While these are large systems, *syllabi*, *courses*, *curriculum*, and *training programs* may also be considered as systems, albeit small. Another significant principle of instructional design is a planned approach to designing the instructional process, events, and material.

Instructional systems design (ISD) model is a systematic process-based approach used to design and develop instructional outcomes, content, learning strategies, and media.

There exist a number of ISD models. While these models may differ in the number of steps or phases, they can all be mapped to three key activities – figuring out the instructional goal, designing and developing the instructional material, and assessing the efficacy of instruction. In this section, we will look at two popular models.

Dick and Carey model

Recall the systems approach in the section introducing the various definitions of instructional design – this is credited to the work of Walter Dick and Lou Carey, in the book, ***The Systematic Design of Instruction*** published in 1978. This model is one of the most influential in instructional design. It is suitable for a variety of context, including workplace training, government institutions, primary and secondary schools, and colleges.

Let's look at each step in this model. It's important to note that the tasks and sub-tasks are not performed in a linear manner; they are interrelated and iterative, as shown in *Figure 1.2*:

Understanding Instructional Design

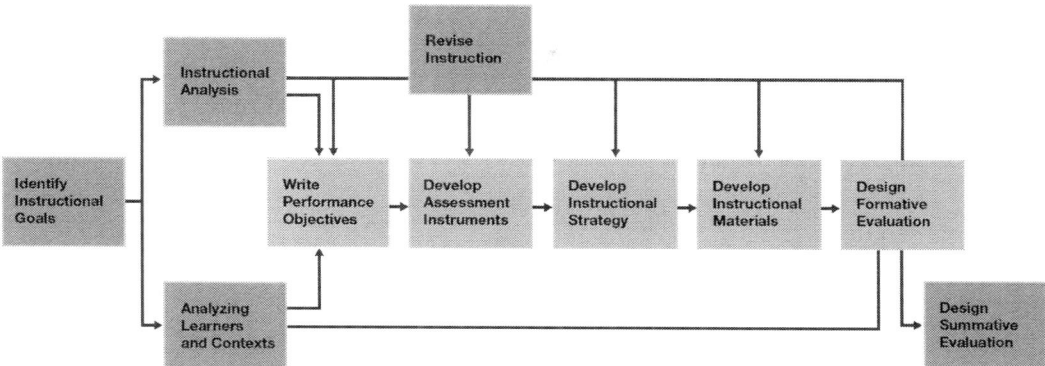

Figure 1.2: Dick and Carey Model

The steps in Dick and Carey model are described as follows:

- *Assess needs to identify goal(s):* This is the first step in the Dick and Carey model. In this step, the purpose of instruction is determined. This means that you ascertain what the learner should be able to do or may do better after the instruction. This is derived through interviews of experts, analysis of past learner performance, or an existing list of goals.

- *Conduct instructional analysis:* Learning something requires the learner to be motivated and have some prior knowledge. The aim of this step is to identify the current levels of knowledge, skills, and attitude of the learner. This is often referred to as entry-level behavior.

- *Analyze learners and contexts:* Where and how will the learners use this instruction? This is the question that is answered through this step. The setting or context in which the learning will occur and will be finally used helps the instructional designers to determine the most effective strategy.

- *Write performance objectives:* Using the information from the analysis (steps 1 to 3), specific outcome statements are written. These statements specify the knowledge to be acquired, or the skill to be mastered. The conditions under which the skill is to be performed and the performance criteria for measuring are also specified in this step.

- *Develop assessment instruments:* This step involves the development of assessment items that measure the learners' ability to perform what is specified in the outcome statements. It is important to ensure that the assessment items match the learning outcomes.

- *Develop instructional strategy:* How will you make sure that the learners achieve the learning outcome? What interventions will you use – in terms of presentation, practice, and feedback? By answering these questions, the instructional designer comes up with an instructional strategy that is in line with the established learning principles and latest research.

- *Develop and select instructional materials:* In this step, instructional materials such as session plans, student and facilitator guides, multimedia modules, videos etc., are either sourced or developed. If the content is not already available, then it is created by the teacher, trainer, or a project team. If the content is available, then that may also be used. The decision to create or use existing material will depend upon two factors – one, whether the existing material is relevant, and two, if there are available resources to create it. The use of existing resources is akin to "content curation" (the practice of identifying, organizing, and collating relevant content) that has become popular amidst the learning and development community these days.

- *Design and conduct the formative evaluation of instruction:* In this model, great emphasis is placed on evaluation *for* learning, also known as formative evaluation. The purpose of this is to use tests as a learning tool to help learners understand the concepts and acquire the skills. It also helps ascertain if the instructional process and instructional material need to be tweaked or modified in any way. The authors reference three types of evaluation as part of this step in the Dick and Carey model. These are one-to-one evaluation, small-group evaluation, and field evaluation.

- *Revise instruction:* This is the final step in the model and involves interpreting the data from the previous step to identify whether the learners faced any difficulties in achieving the learning outcomes. Any issues that are identified are analyzed and the instructional strategy is revised, so that the instructional material or the instructional process becomes more effective.

- *Design and conduct summative evaluation:* Summative evaluation is the evaluation *of* learning and is different from formative evaluation. In other words, it is conducted to judge the learner's performance and award grades after the learning process is complete. This isn't formally considered as part of the design process, because an independent evaluator is expected to administer this sort of evaluation.

ADDIE model

The **ADDIE model** is yet another framework that is used to design instructional material. ADDIE is an acronym for Analysis, Design, Development, Implementation, and Evaluation.

Let's go through this model in detail. The five phases in the model are depicted in *Figure 1.3*, which is adapted to include the variables and constants that was explained earlier:

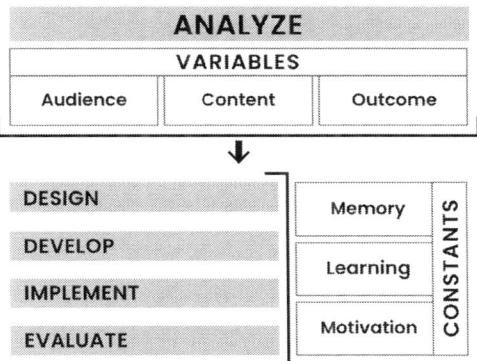

Figure 1.3: ADDIE Model (Adapted version)

Let's look at the five phases, described as follows:

- **Analysis:** The purpose of designing instruction is to facilitate the learners to move from their current state to a goal state. The **Analysis** phase helps in specifying these two states, and hence, is the foundation of the instructional design process. The needs analysis, audience analysis, and content analysis are completed in this phase. If the instructional material is for the workplace skills or vocational training, then a task analysis is also performed. These activities help the instructional designer to identify the knowledge or skills gaps, define the performance or learning problem, specify the learning outcomes, and detail out the characteristics of the learner, such as entry-level knowledge and behavior, motivation to learn, challenges they may be facing, and so on. The output of this phase is called the **Training Needs Analysis (TNA)** or **Learning Needs Analysis (LNA)**, which then forms the input for the Design phase. *The chapter, Analyzing Learning Need* will address this phase in detail.

- **Design:** The **Design** phase involves using the output from the Analysis phase to outline the instructional material and instructional events that will help the learners achieve the desired goal. The output of this phase is a blueprint that addresses the content scope, content flow, and the instructional approach to be adopted, and the strategies for evaluating the learner. The evaluation or assessment strategies are a vital component in the blueprint. The output of this phase is the High-level Design or Program Outline, and the Detailed Design Document. This document serves as the input for creating all the instructional materials. The following chapters, *Designing the Outline, Defining Learning Outcomes and Designing Instructional Material* will address the program outline, learning outcomes, and instructional approach, while the chapter, *Assessment Strategies,* will address the assessment strategies.

- **Development:** With the commencement of this phase, the instructional designers move into the production mode. Prior to this phase, the key tasks are researching, surveying, and ideating. In the **development** phase, they begin creating all the instructional materials that have been identified as part of the blueprint. What materials the instructional designers develop will depend upon where they are working (*Table 1.3*). If they are writing books, they would mostly be subject matter experts who will collaborate with the editors and graphic designers. In the case of online learning material, instructional designers will need to collaborate with the subject matter experts, instructional design reviewers, editors, graphic designers, and programmers. This phase is addressed in the chapter, *Developing Instructional Material.*

- **Implementation:** The **Implementation** phase refers to the actual delivery of the instruction. If the instructional material is for classroom use, then it will be used by the teacher or facilitator within a classroom environment. This is applicable to course books, lessons and session plans, online modules, and videos that are used by the teacher in a physical classroom. If the instructional material is designed for self-paced online learning, then it is hosted using the software known as the learning platform. Sometimes the solution will include both the online and the classroom components – this is known as a blended approach. Lately, the virtual teacher-led training has become common in schools, colleges and the workplace. The implementation phase in such situations will then involve the use of a collaboration tool. The chapter, *Delivery Strategies* will address all these situations in detail.

- **Evaluation: Evaluation** phase measures the effectiveness and efficacy of the instructional material by evaluating learner understanding and achievement, and by evaluating the instructional process and instructional materials. Learner evaluation is of two types – **formative evaluation**, which occurs as part of the learning process, and **summative evaluation**, which occurs after the learning process. Evaluation of workplace learning takes it a step further, and involves evaluating learning transfer, and calculating the **return on investment (ROI)**. Evaluation occurs throughout the instructional design process - within phases, between phases, and after implementation. The input from this is used to fill gaps, if any, in the instructional materials. Initial ADDIE models were linear. Of late, however, the ADDIE model has become iterative. This phase is covered in *Chapter 8, Assessment Strategies.*

> Note: Here is an interesting fact about ADDIE. In the year, 2003, Michael Molenda, a professor at Indiana University, researched and concluded that the term ADDIE is not the name of any specific framework but is an informal reference to the systematic approach to creating instructional materials.

Table 1.3 provides an overview of the instructional material that is created in different industries/institutions:

Industry/Institution	Instructional Material
Publishing	Course books
	Reference books
Multimedia Companies (K-12)	ICT-integrated lesson plans
	Online modules
	Videos
	Learning Apps
Higher Education	Curriculum
	Online courses
	Videos
Corporate Organizations	Online modules
	Videos
	Session plans (virtual and classroom)
	Presentations
Vocational Training Institutes	Curriculum
	Session plans (Virtual and Classroom)
	Facilitator guide
	Participant handbooks
	Presentations
	Online modules

Table 1.3: Instructional material mapped to industries/institutions

> Note: There's a misconception among many that instructional design is applicable only to the creation of online learning or e-learning. This belief perhaps developed because instructional design became popular with the advent of computers and the Internet. However, in the book, The Systematic Design of Instruction, the authors have noted that instructional systems design is a generic planning process applicable to print, video, and interactive material.

ADDIE and Dick & Carey model – a comparison

As you can see in *Table 1.4*, all the tasks that are performed as part of the Dick and Carey Model are also performed in the ADDIE model. The latter combines certain tasks to make it a five-phase process. The fact that it appears shorter and is addressed using a mnemonic, could be the reason for its popularity over the Dick and Carey model. Refer to *Table 1.4* that compares ADDIE with the Dick & Carey model:

ADDIE	Dick & Carey
Analysis	Assess needs to identify goal(s)
	Conduct instructional analysis
	Analyze learners and contexts
Design	Write performance objectives
	Develop assessment instruments
	Develop instructional strategy
Development	Develop and select instructional materials
Implementation	Design and conduct the formative evaluation of instruction
	Revise instruction
Evaluation	Design and conduct summative evaluation

Table 1.4: Mapping ADDIE with Dick & Carey

Other models

There are other instructional design models too, such as the Kemp Design model, **Successive Approximation model** (**SAM**), and Rapid Prototyping. There are variations between these in terms of stages and tasks. However, in essence, they are similar because all models focus on the learner, and what the learner will be able to accomplish after instruction.

The chapters in this book are structured around the ADDIE model. It is one of the most popular models that is applied widely – for different audience profile and varied media – and has been found to be very useful for instructional planning and development.

> Note: A study conducted by Rouhollah Khodabandelou and Siti Akmar Abu Samah published in 2012, concluded that the ADDIE model was one of the four most commonly-used instructional design models for the design of online learning material.

Instructional design versus design thinking

An introductory chapter on instructional design is not complete without the mention of design thinking, which is a buzzword these days. In fact, there are numerous articles, which discuss how the design thinking process can be applied to instructional design. However, the ADDIE model is quite akin to design thinking (*Figure 1.4*). Let us see how.

Think about this. You have an elderly diabetic person coming over for dinner. What would you cook? The best thing to do would be to find out what the guest can or cannot eat and plan your menu accordingly. And if that is what you would do, then you are clearly applying design thinking. Empathizing with the user is the cornerstone of the design thinking process, and in this situation, your effort at finding out what the guest can and cannot eat, and then planning the menu is empathizing. This is quite similar to the instructional design process, wherein you design the instructional material that is learner-centric. It is just that instructional design never received even a fraction of the publicity that design thinking has been receiving these days. Perhaps it is because the former falls in the domain of educators and trainers, people who are not necessarily very marketing savvy! Refer to *Figure 1.4* that illustrates the difference between the ADDIE model and Design Thinking:

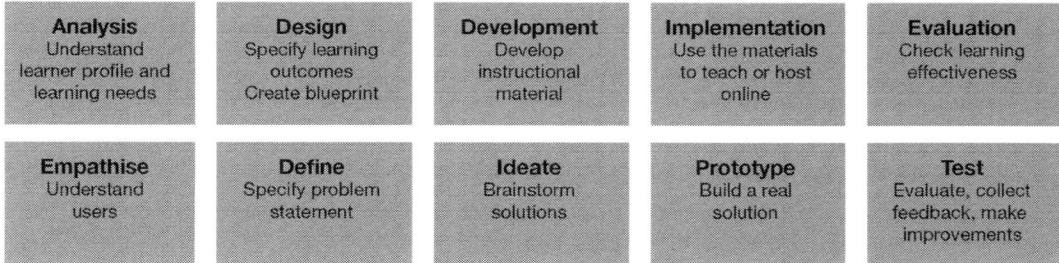

Figure 1.4: ADDIE versus Design Thinking

Conclusion

The teaching-learning process, in recent times, has undergone a change. From being teacher-driven, passive, and individualistic, the learning experiences are becoming learner-driven, active, and collaborative. The instructional design processes and models help us design the material that meets these changed requirements. The ADDIE model provides a systematic process for designing instructional material. There are other models for designing instruction, such as Dick and Carey, Kemp, SAM, Rapid Prototyping etc., but the ADDIE model is more commonly applied.

In the next chapter, we will delve into the first phase of the ADDIE model, which is Analysis. The chapter will address how learning 'needs analysis' is completed for workplace learning and vocational skills, and for K-12, and higher education. In addition, the chapter will present some frameworks that help in understanding the target learner, be it the school students, the youth, or the working professionals.

Points to remember

- Instructional design is the systematic process of analyzing the learner needs and developing the learning material to address these needs.
- It teaches us to analyze the context in every learning situation; the context being three variables – the audience (learner), the content to be taught, and the learning outcome.
- Instructional design, as a discipline, is guided by three constants, which are the scientific principles of memory, learning, and motivation.
- Instructional design adopts a systematic approach to the design of instructional material and interventions, thereby ensuring instructional effectiveness.
- This field is of great significance as all kinds of learners – whether in K-12, higher education, vocational skills, or corporate training – increasingly veer towards multi-modal and self-determined learning.
- The ADDIE model is a popular framework adopted by instructional designers for designing the learning material. ADDIE is an acronym where each letter represents a phase, as follows:
    - **Analysis** of learners, learning needs, and learning outcomes.
    - **Design** the blueprint, which includes performance outcomes, program outline, instructional approach, and evaluation strategies.
    - **Development** of instructional material, such as course books, facilitator guides, student guides, session plans, and multimedia or online material.

- o **Implementation** of the instructional plan using the instructional material that is developed or curated.

- o **Evaluation** of the learner performance and instructional effectiveness.

Multiple choice questions

1. **Learning material and learning experiences in the contemporary technology-developed world must be _____. Select the correct option.**

    a) Learner-centric

    b) Content-centric

    c) Teacher-driven

    d) Media-driven

2. **Learning outcome statements are written in which phase of the ADDIE model?**

    a) Implement

    b) Evaluate

    c) Design

    d) Develop

    e) Analyze

3. **Which of these is NOT an output of the Development phase?**

    a) Textbook Chapter

    b) Online Module

    c) K-12 Lesson Plan

    d) Instructor Guide

    e) Program Outline

4. **Which of these is NOT an instructional design model?**

    a) Dick & Carey

    b) Design Thinking

    c) Kemp

    d) Rapid Prototyping

    e) ADDIE

Answers

1. a
2. c
3. e
4. b

Questions

1. Describe instructional design from three different perspectives.
2. Explain the various stages of the ADDIE model.
3. Why is instructional design referred to as a systems approach?
4. Illustrate how the ADDIE model is similar to the Design Thinking approach.

Key terms

- *Pedagogy:* The method and practice of teaching, especially as an academic subject or theoretical concept.
- *ID Variables:* The components in an instructional situation that change based on the context.
- *ID Constants:* The principles of memory, learning, and motivation that drive the design of instructional material.
- *Analogy:* A comparison between one thing and another, typically for the purpose of explanation or clarification.
- *Instructional systems design:* A systematic process-based approach used to design and develop instructional outcomes, content, learning strategies, and media.
- *Content Curation:* The process of finding, collating, organizing, and sharing relevant content to meet a specific learning outcome.
- *Formative Evaluation:* The assessment **for** learning, which is part of the learning process and meant to help learners acquire skills and understand concepts.
- *Summative Evaluation:* The assessment **of** learning, which is administered after the learning process to award grades and scores.

CHAPTER 2
Analyzing Learning Need

Introduction

Rita sat in her history class. She really wanted to listen to what her teacher was explaining, but she just couldn't focus. She was a conscientious student who tried very hard to concentrate. But then, she got distracted and started thinking about the movie, BIG starring Tom Hanks, which she saw the previous night.

In this movie, a wish turns a 12-year-old boy into a 30-year-old man physically. This forces the child-man to get a job and mingle in the world of adults. So, he heads to New York City and starts work in a toy company. Surprisingly, the job he gets with the toy manufacturer is perfect, because being a kid himself (cognitively), he provides valuable insight into the toys that kids would like.

That's when it struck Rita that if teachers could become younger, you know like kids all over again, they would understand why children got distracted and perhaps do something to address it.

It is funny how she thought only kids her age get bored in the classroom. The other day she overheard her father, a manager with a finance company, complaining about how he had to sit through a boring and completely useless training on cultural diversity. He said that the training covered everything that everybody already knew – and that the issue to be tackled wasn't the lack of understanding about diversity, but with not being sensitive enough.

Some learners love certain subjects and may dislike others. Some may find a topic boring, while the same may hold great appeal for others. This is explained by Howard Gardner, as the *Multiple Intelligences Theory*, according to which, our interest or lack of it for a certain subject may be innate. Though this has been criticized by some educationists, there is a lesson here. Shouldn't teachers, instructional designers, and educators reflect on why learners lose interest in learning and find ways and techniques to generate interest? Shouldn't we be challenging ourselves to design learning in such a manner that we capture the attention of both – the most ardent fan, and the bored-out-of-wits cynic? Why should learning be either effective or engaging when we can make it both? If you are passionate about teaching, you will agree that this can be achieved regardless of whether it is a textbook, an online learning module, a blended learning program, a video tutorial, or a physical classroom session. To achieve this, the ADDIE model includes the analysis phase, which is the focus of this chapter.

Structure

In this chapter, we will discuss the following topics:

- Significance of the analysis phase of the ADDIE model
- Analysis for workplace skills and analysis in education
- DACUM approach for job analysis
- Piaget's theory of cognitive development
- William Perry's cognitive and ethical development theory

Objectives

After studying this chapter, you will be able to describe the significance of the analysis phase. In addition, you will understand how adults, youth, and children differ as learners. Finally, you will learn about the following theories and frameworks that help us to analyze learner needs – andragogy, DACUM approach, Piaget's theory of cognitive development, and William Perry's cognitive and ethical development theory.

Significance of analysis

Here is a scenario. Suppose an institution approaches an instructional designer to help them design an English Communication Skills course for the hearing impaired. This could be part of a workplace readiness program, which will address other skills along with communication, so that the hearing-impaired students may be gainfully employed. Are you wondering how an instructional designer, who is gifted with the ability to speak and hear, can do justice to this? A valid question, no doubt. But this drawback – not knowing the learner – is exactly why analysis is included as a key phase in the ADDIE methodology.

In the analysis phase, the instructional designer will try to understand the target learners. She will need to spend time with the learners, observe them, and even attend sign language classes. This experience will help the instructional designer to understand how those who are hearing-impaired use other faculties to compensate for the lack of their hearing ability. It will also challenge her to identify strategies that will exploit the strengths of the hearing-impaired. For instance, the target audience makes up for the lack of verbal skills with their heightened *visual* skills. This insight can help the instructional designer to design the instructional material using several visual aids, signs, and symbols. It will also help her scope the content by picking a minimum vocabulary, which is relevant to their everyday life and will be needed to communicate via messaging and emails.

We saw in *Chapter 1, Understanding Instructional Design*, that there are three *variables* in instructional design. These are the audience, content, and learning outcomes (*Figure 2.1*). The very fact that these are variables, means that these differ from context to context. The analysis phase helps us understand these variables for a specific context. Of the three variables, the learning outcomes and the target audience will be broadly known. The learning outcome may be a broad statement like a goal (English Communication Skills in the preceding scenario), and instructional designers have to break this down into smaller and specific outcomes. With regard to the target audience, instructional designers will have to identify information, such as their prior knowledge, motivation levels, and constraints. These two variables will then help the instructional designer to scope the content to address the specific learning outcome.

Refer to *Figure 2.1* that illustrates the ADDIE model:

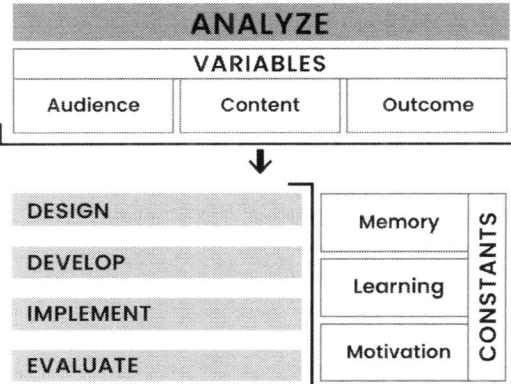

Figure 2.1: ADDIE Model (Adapted version)

As school students, we learn a lot of things, which we are not expected to put to use. In college, we select a specific subject and focus on learning everything about that. As adults, we invest our time and effort to learn something that will help us navigate through life.

Example 2.1: Suppose a 60-year-old lady wants to learn how to access the Internet using a smart phone. She will obviously not want to learn about the evolution of computers or the definition of a web browser. Her focus will be to learn only the procedure to access the Internet using the smart phone. On the contrary, when school students in Grade 5 learn about the Internet, the content will address the evolution of the Internet, the definition of web browser and many other concepts related to the Internet along with the procedure to access it.

Example 2.1 illustrates that learning a specific skill to perform a real-world task is very different from pursuing formal education. Therefore, the analysis process for workplace training and vocational skills differs from the analysis process for school and college education.

Analysis for workplace skills

Do you recall the process of Design Thinking that was addressed in *Chapter 1, Understanding Instructional Design*? Some educationists differentiate between instructional design and Design Thinking on the premise that the former is a systems-driven approach, while the latter is a human-centered approach. However, if we ignore semantics, we will find that the two are not very different. The Design Thinking process is based upon three basic principles, *empathy*, *observation* and *user-centeredness*. The analysis phase of the ADDIE model is also geared towards understanding audience characteristics and their environment. This is done by interviewing, observing and listening to them with empathy and understanding, so that the solution we design is learner-centric.

Here is an interesting anecdote to emphasize the point of user-centeredness. If you live in a city, and it has a metro rail as a form of public transport, you would have seen a metro map. Unlike regular maps that focus on distance, details, and geographical accuracy, this one resembles a circuit diagram. The credit to this goes to Harry Beck, an engineering draftsman, who designed London's subway map in this manner. The neat, clear, and color-coded crisscrossing lines were designed with such simplicity and elegance that it has become the template for transport maps all over the world. These maps are easily understood by users, though we cannot be sure if Harry Beck did a conscious end-user profiling. But there is definitely a lesson here for all instructional designers – that it is important to design your learning material keeping the target audience in mind.

Both workplace professionals and vocational students enroll for a course to acquire practical skills that they can use in the workplace. However, there is a distinction between the two because the workplace professional is more mature, experienced, and motivated than the vocational student. In the following section, we will look at how we can better understand both these categories of learners.

Understanding an adult learner

Firstly, adult learners are tough and demanding customers, and the most unforgiving. Rarely will the *carrot and stick* approach work with them. You have to give them what they need and not what *you think* they need, and that too in a package which appeals to them. Conducting a thorough and robust analysis of the audience and their learning need is, therefore, imperative.

Secondly, adult learners are set in their ways – they are not as malleable as young students. The analysis phase will help you zero-in on the most appropriate methodology – the *how* and, may be, even the *where* of training. For instance, if the target audience is young, you may want to use language that is conversational, but if the target audience is experienced, or slightly elderly professionals, they may just view such language as frivolous. Similarly, the sales and marketing staff, by nature, are competitive – they must always achieve targets, which makes them good candidates for game-based learning. On the other hand, engineers work with diagrams and blueprints, so one should consider including that as an instructional strategy for them. The analysis phase will help you uncover characteristics, challenges, and constraints of the target audience. These findings will work as input when you get into the design phase of the ADDIE methodology.

Adult learner traits are captured succinctly by Malcolm Knowles through the theory of *andragogy*. According to this theory, the following principles drive adult learning:

- Adults need to be involved in the planning and evaluation of their instruction.
- Experience (including mistakes) provides the basis for learning activities.
- Adults are most interested in learning subjects that have immediate relevance and impact on their job or personal life.
- Adult learning is problem-centric rather than content-oriented.

Finally, adult learners like to learn only when the material is relevant to their work and job responsibilities. Even theory and concepts must be connected in some way with practical application at work. This brings us to a very significant part of the analysis phase, which is *job analysis* (also called *task analysis*). Job analysis involves systematically identifying the fundamental elements of a job, and the knowledge and skills required for the job's performance. The information gleaned from this activity is used to develop learning outcomes (the second variable) and scoping the *content* (the third variable).

You can conduct audience analysis through interviews or by administering a questionnaire. *Example 2.2* depicts a sample audience analysis questionnaire for workplace training:

Example 2.2: Questionnaire for audience analysis (Workplace Training)

1. **What is the average experience of the target audience in designing and developing content?**
    a) Less than 2 years
    b) 2–4 years
    c) More than 4 years

2. **How many of them have attended some form of training in Instructional Design in the past?**
    a) All
    b) None
    c) Some

3. **How many in the target audience have experience in conducting classroom training sessions?**
    a) All
    b) None
    c) Some

4. **What deliverables/outputs do you create as part of the content development process?**
    a) Content/Program Outline
    b) Design Document
    c) Approach Note
    d) Storyboards for Online learning
    e) ILT Materials (Presentations, Participant Guide, and Facilitator Guide)

5. **In what format(s) is the training currently rendered at your workplace?**
    a) Classroom Training
    b) Traditional E-Learning Modules

c) Explainer Videos
d) Job-Aids
e) Any Other (Please Specify)

Challenges in workplace analysis

When you conduct analysis for workplace skills, you face a few challenges. It is important to be aware of these, as it will help you to be prepared to face the challenges. If there is standard training that all roles are required to go through in a company, then scoping the content will be a challenge. For instance, suppose that a financial institution needs its employees to be trained and be sensitive to money laundering; the content for the same will be scoped differently for different departments and roles. For example, while a training company would want new employees from the instructional design, project management, and graphics departments to understand the **development life cycle** (**DLC**) of a project, the instructional design and instructional writing components of the training will be mandatory only for the instructional design department. Similarly, instructional designers may be trained in the basics of visualization, but the graphic designers will need to undergo an intensive training in the same. It is important to keep these factors in mind when you conduct analysis for workplace learning.

A second challenge that instructional designers face when conducting analysis is the difficulty in understanding some of the terms used by the **subject matter experts** (**SME**), because they lack subject matter expertise. For instance, in an oil and gas company, the terms *upstream* and *downstream* will be used frequently; in the information technology sector, the terms *artificial intelligence, machine learning,* and *deep learning* imply different things, though an instructional designer may club all these terms together. Therefore, it is imperative that when instructional designers visit a client site for conducting analysis, they must be well prepared with the common jargons used in the industry.

Finally, another significant challenge is the fact that analysis for workplace skills is not a one-time task or a simple linear process. It is iterative, and the instructional designers must be prepared to go back and forth and revisit their findings more than once. And, if the organization is a global one, then the entire analysis phase may take a month or more to complete. Cutting corners or fast-tracking this phase may result in rework later.

Example 2.3 depicts the findings after completing the analysis for an airline. Note how complex the requirements are – the number of varied roles, varying experience within a role, and the different subjects that need to be addressed as part of training. It is important to document all such requirements as part of the analysis phase in order to design effective workplace training.

Example 2.3: Findings from an analysis for a project

Overview

EAGLE Airlines, a leading international airline, based out of the Far East, is planning to expand its operations globally. It has also purchased new state-of-the-art aircrafts. To be able to maintain the same level of customer service, the airline wants to train its existing and new employees to maintain their on-the-job high-level performance, and in the process, make EAGLE Airlines the number one airline in the world.

Training needs

The airline wants to identify current skill gaps amongst all its employees. However, the priority is the employees in primary roles, such as pilots and cabin crew. They are looking at the solution provider to recommend a design that will be most effective, given the busy travel schedules of pilots and cabin crew. The same training will be extended to other roles later. The airline wants its employees to be up to date with the new requirements within a year. Apart from training in customer service, the airline has emphasized the need for a special course on phonetics and pronunciation of customer-oriented English words, so that the crew is sensitive to the significance of appropriate pronunciation in providing good customer service.

Audience and content

The average age of employees at EAGLE Airlines is around 25 years. While pilots have an aeronautical engineering degree, a large percentage of the cabin crew has only high-school background. Upon joining, cabin crew members attend boot camp training, and EAGLE Airlines ensures they have a minimum period of at least 10 days of refresher training every year. The employees are extremely motivated to learn and perform. They are hired from the main hub in the Far East, and hence they are very adept in the native language, but while speaking with non-native customers in English, they are not so comfortable. The curriculum is to address the following:

- Pilot and cabin crew training: Airline detail features, functions, codes, standard operating procedure, rosters.

- Aircraft features: How each component works, safety mechanics, the dos and don'ts. Training to be for pilots, and certain topics for the cabin crew.

- Cabin crew training: Long haul and short haul flights, food and beverages, inflight entertainment, customer needs, senior citizen and baby care.

- English language: Phonetics, pronunciation, and usage; not grammar.

The training is to be tied to certification. Employees must pass the certification exam at three stages. The outcome should be related to further training, or placement under a mentor for a fixed period, or placed directly on the job.

Understanding the vocational student

A **vocational student** is mostly a young learner who is neither a child, nor an adult. They are at the cusp of adulthood and tend to display traits common to both teenagers and adults. For instance, they want autonomy to learn and don't like to be controlled. At the same time, they expect support and feedback from the system. They prefer self-directed learning, but also want to be guided by the system. One prominent characteristic of the vocational student, which has a significant bearing on how instruction is designed, is that they expect that the time spent on learning will help them to get a job.

While these universal traits may give us some direction, a more in-depth analysis is required because the vocational students are not a homogeneous audience. They may vary in age and have differing educational background. In India, there are added challenges in the form of socio-cultural diversities and the preference of students to pursue a formal college education over vocational skills. The analysis phase helps the instructional designers to understand such challenges.

Example 2.4 depicts a sample audience analysis questionnaire for vocational training.

Example 2.4: Questionnaire for audience analysis (Vocational Training)

A - Demographic Profile

Age

- 16-18
- 18-21
- 21-24
- 24+

Economic background

- Economically backward
- Lower middle class
- Upper middle class

Educational background

- 8th grade
- 10th grade
- 12th grade
- Graduate

B- Psychographic Profile

Motivation to learn

- Low
- Satisfactory
- High

Goal Orientation

- Low
- Satisfactory
- High

C - Learning Proficiency

Reading

- Low
- Satisfactory
- High

Writing

- Low
- Satisfactory
- High

Listening

- Low
- Satisfactory
- High

Doing

- Low
- Satisfactory
- High

Job analysis

As we read earlier, the job/task analysis helps instructional designers understand the knowledge and skills that are required to perform a certain job role. This helps them to scope the content. In order to complete this activity, instructional designers must work closely with **subject matter experts** (**SME**) to understand the domain. During the interaction between the instructional designer and the SME, the instructional designer must go through the content from a learner's perspective. The SME, on the other hand, should go through each step to complete a task, and explain what knowledge and skills are needed to complete the task. The instructional designer must quiz the SME on various points, such as misconceptions surrounding a concept, critical oversights that novices might make, and best practices for completing a task. This is significant because a lot of such knowledge may be tacit and should be brought out clearly, so that it may be included in the instructional material.

DACUM, short for Developing A Curriculum, is a quick and effective job analysis technique that may be applied to identify the learning outcomes, and scope the content. The DACUM process is used to determine the competencies that should be addressed in a training curriculum for a specific occupation. DACUMs are used to develop job profiles for all types of occupations, including top-level managers and specialized jobs.

DACUM is based on three premises:

(1) Using expert workers to describe their jobs.

(2) Describing jobs vis-à-vis the competencies or tasks of the successful workers in that occupation perform.

(3) Detailing out the specific knowledge, skills, attitudes, and the tools required by workers in order to correctly perform their job.

This process, as shown in *Figure 2.2*, may be facilitated by instructional designers in the following manner:

- *Define job profile:* Facilitate expert workers to analyze their own profile for identifying critical tasks, time-consuming tasks, and training needs.

- *Validate job profile:* Get the tasks and training needs identified by expert workers and ratified by peers and management for workplace professionals. The same may be validated by the **sector skill council** (**SSC**) members for vocational training.

- *Create skill matrix:* Based on the information derived from phase one and two, create a skill matrix with SME help to scope the content, and design the curriculum.

Refer to *Figure 2.2* that illustrates the DACUM approach:

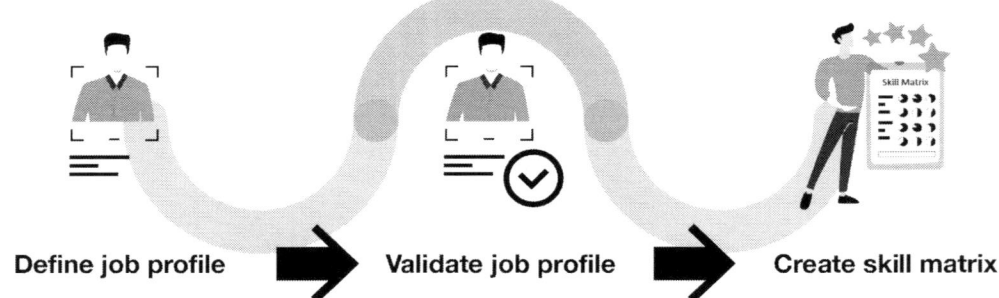

Figure 2.2:DACUM Approach

Example 2.5 displays a sample questionnaire for conducting the job/task analysis:

Example 2.5: Questionnaire for job analysis

1. What is the nature of the task?
    - Procedural
    - Mechanical/Technical
    - Interpersonal
    - Cognitive
    - Any Other
2. What domain knowledge is needed to perform the task? For example, instructional design, software design, computer networking, management and so on.
3. What skills are needed in the performance of the task?
    - Decision-making
    - Creativity
    - Problem Solving
    - Collaboration
    - Time management
    - Adaptability
    - Any Other

4. How frequently is the task performed?
   - Daily
   - Weekly
   - Monthly
   - Annually
5. How critical is the task to the performance of the job?
   - Very critical
   - Somewhat critical
   - Not Critical
6. How is the task performed?
   - Individually
   - In collaboration
7. If this task is a subset of a set of collective tasks, what is the relationship between the various tasks? Illustrate this visually.
8. What is the consequence if the task is performed incorrectly or is not performed at all?
   - Customer dissatisfaction
   - Legal issues
   - Safety concerns
   - Any Other

Job analysis is relevant in defining the learning outcomes and content scope for both workplace training and vocational skilling. In workplace training, this activity helps in designing the training for new recruits in a certain role, or for performance improvement of the existing employees. Very often, it is assumed that the cause for all the performance issues in the workplace is a lack of skill or knowledge. However, the solution to every performance problem is not always training. To figure out whether the solution is indeed training, you must get the big picture. Needs analysis in the professional workplace helps determine the root cause for a performance gap. Sometimes, the cause can be factors other than the lack of skill or knowledge, such as cynicism, role ambiguity, inadequate support, inefficient resources, or process lacunae. Such causes may require interventions, other than training. These interventions could be in the form of one-to-one discussions, incentives or process-tweaking. You must be absolutely certain that you have nailed the cause – else you will end up creating a training that nobody uses, which does not address the performance problem.

> **Note: Instructional design is context specific. The example questionnaires included in this chapter are meant to give you an idea about what sort of questions should be asked during the analysis phase. Instructional designers must create a customized questionnaire with questions that suit the context.**

Analysis in education

Unlike workplace skills, school and college education is not about performing tasks. It is an investment by modern democracies to improve the life of its citizens and ensure a stable society. Hence, a big part of the analysis phase is completed by government-appointed committees. However, this does not mean that instructional designers and educators working in K-12 or higher education do not have to conduct any analysis. They still have to understand their audience if they are to make the instructional process and materials learner-centric. Let's see how.

Higher education

The curriculum for higher education is highly influenced by job prospects and the economic environment. Furthermore, this environment changes over time and between contexts. Thus, the program or discipline designed by any institution follows the policies laid down by a curriculum team after a detailed analysis of the international environment, job prospects, and skill demand within a country and globally, as shown in *Figure 2.3*:

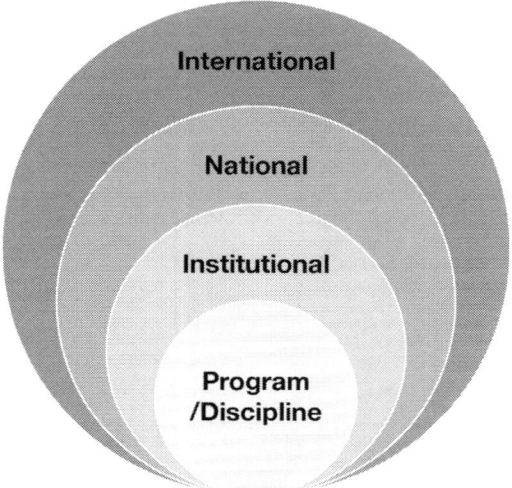

Figure 2.3: Higher Education Determinants

The curriculum team is made up of policy makers, and academic and industry experts who will detail out the following:

- Student characteristics at entry level
- Student, program, and institution goals
- External influences on the discipline
- Current industry trends and requirements
- Learning resources

Those who design and develop the learning material for higher education must treat the curriculum as a starting point and take forward the analysis. It is important to understand that in higher education, the learning goal goes beyond the development of disciplinary expertise or technical knowledge and must include the development of workplace skills and attributes for independent study and lifelong learning. These must be seamlessly embedded into the course materials, and the complete gamut of skills and attributes should be reflected at the program level.

In most cases, a majority of those who enroll in higher education institutions are what we call the *youth learner*. Understanding and profiling these learners, vis-à-vis their personality, values, exposure to independent learning, motivation levels to take the program, interests, hopes and aspirations in career and life, and the challenges in pursuing a full-time, part-time, or distance learning course must be carefully considered as part of the analysis. Also, given that higher educational institutions are increasingly moving towards a blended mode of delivery – using classroom and online formats, instructional designers must analyze the appropriate blend, and segregate topics into those that will be delivered online, and those that will be delivered in the traditional classroom format.

William Perry (1913–1998), a psychologist and researcher at the Harvard Graduate School of Education, developed a theory of cognitive and ethical development among college students, according to which, college students go through four phases of mental and moral development. This theory provides great insights into understanding the traits of students in higher education, and how best to address them – by helping students to not just acquire domain knowledge but also develop their thinking abilities for them to become lifelong learners. The four phases are described as follows:

- *Dualism:* Students view knowledge as truth that they receive from their professors in the form of facts, and theories with right and wrong answers. Learning in this phase involves taking notes, memorizing the material, and taking tests and exams.
- *Multiplicity:* In this phase, knowledge becomes a matter of opinion, and professors are no longer the authorities with the right answers, and there is

no way to determine what is right. There is ambiguity, and knowledge is no longer equated with certainty. Students begin to question authority and may conclude that no absolute truth exists, only perspectives and perceptions.

- *Relativism:* In this phase, students recognize that knowledge is contextual and what you know about something is influenced by your experiences, perspectives, and forms of inquiry. Students begin to understand that what you know or claim to know must be supported with evidence.

- *Commitment in Relativism:* In this stage, the brain appreciates ambiguity as a quality and students begin to recognize that reasonable answers often depend upon the contexts and value systems in which the problems occur and are amenable to investigation. It is this final stage that professors guide their students to achieve, so that when they go out in the uncertain world, they will define their own values and identity, make educated choices, evaluate options, create new knowledge, and become lifelong learners.

K-12

Just like in higher education, the analysis phase for K-12 is also completed by an academic team that develops policy documents and a broad curriculum. By and large, this team puts together a report that includes the following:

- Key issues and trends in the specific content area
- K-12 program philosophy
- K-12 program, grade-level outcomes, and course goals
- Resource materials to assist with program implementation
- Assessment items and instruments to measure student progress

Note: Since outcome analysis and content analysis are completed by a different entity for K-12 and higher education, instructional designers must read policy documents that address the findings and follow the broad guidelines specified in these.

The fact that a curriculum guide is available, should not be viewed by teachers and instructional designers as the culmination of the analysis phase. On the contrary, they should use this as a starting point for the phase, and they must understand the cognitive abilities of students, which vary across grades. While the curriculum takes care of this in terms of content scoping and broad guidelines for content treatment, the onus is on the teacher or instructional designer to present and explain the content using age-appropriate strategies, as shown in *Example 2.6*:

Example 2.6: Suppose you are teaching Calculus to senior school students, who are on the threshold of selecting a career. It is not adequate to simply explain the concepts; you must figure out ways in which you make the topic relevant to the students – connect it to various occupations and sectors because the learning need of students at this stage goes beyond an understanding of concepts to understanding their relevance and applicability in the professional world. Therefore, explaining how this concept is used by financial professionals, scientists, engineers, architects, statisticians, and other professionals is as important as the explanation of the concept itself.

Age-related differences

A child aged eight can comprehend that the earth is shaped like a sphere, but a child aged four cannot. The difference in cognitive abilities of children has been addressed by Swiss psychologist, Jean Piaget, in his theory of cognitive development. How Piaget came up with the theory is a rather interesting story in itself. Apparently, Piaget was working at the Binet Institute in the 1920s, where he was given the responsibility of developing French versions of English intelligence tests. While doing this, he became intrigued with the reasons children gave for their wrong answers to the questions that required logical thinking. He believed that these incorrect answers revealed important differences between the thinking of adults and children. This led him to systematically observe his own three children over a period of time and come up with the theory of cognitive development that included four distinct stages –(1) the sensorimotor stage, from birth to age 2; (2) the preoperational stage, from age 2 to about age 7; (3) the concrete operational stage, from age 7 to 11; and (4) the formal operational stage, which begins in adolescence and spans into adulthood. The cognitive abilities of children evolve through these stages, described as follows:

- *Sensorimotor (Birth – 2 years):* During this stage, an infant's knowledge of the world is limited to his or her sensory perceptions and motor activities. Behaviors are limited to simple motor responses caused by sensory stimuli. Children acquire object permanence, in other words, memory. This is the understanding that objects in the environment exist regardless of whether they perceive them or not.

- *Preoperational (2 – 7 years):* In this stage, a child learns to use language. During this stage, children do not yet understand concrete logic, cannot mentally manipulate information, and are unable to understand the point of view of other people. They recognize patterns, memorize small poems, and make simple observations, but have difficulty separating magic beliefs from reality.

- *Concrete Operational (7 – 11 years):* During this stage, children gain a better understanding of mental operations. Children begin thinking logically about concrete events but have difficulty understanding abstract or hypothetical concepts. They understand logic and reason and are able to organize their thoughts. However, they cannot handle abstract reasoning, or visualize concepts beyond two dimensions.

- *Formal Operational Stage (Adolescence to Adulthood):* As students enter this stage, they gain the ability to think in an abstract manner, the ability to combine and classify items in a more sophisticated way, and the capacity for higher-order reasoning. They are able to see beyond "right" or "wrong" on complex issues. They can also generate abstract ideas, multiple hypotheses, and possible outcomes. It is important to note that formal operational thinking emerges gradually and not all at once.

Contextual differences

Learning is a process, and not a single event that is confined to the classroom. This process takes place in an environment, and is influenced by various physical, social, cultural, economic, and political factors. Any learning intervention that fails to take these into consideration is bound to be unsuccessful in the long run. The world that we inhabit is diverse and instructional designers must take this diversity into account when they design learning material, especially for students in the lower grades.

Consider a lesson on balanced diet for students in Grade 5. While such a lesson will be similar in terms of the key content that is covered, (proteins, vitamins, minerals, fiber, and carbohydrates) across cultures for the same age, it will be distinct in the content that is added to exemplify the concept because food habits vary from region to region, and across cultures. This is just one example of diversity. *Table 2.1* shows a list of diversities that can have considerable impact on the learning experience of children:

Difference	Explanation
Socio-cultural diversity	Eating steamed rice with curry for lunch may be normal in one culture but alien in another.
	Children in cities will relate to the concept of junk food, like burgers and pizza, while those in remote areas that are untouched by modern life will not be able to relate with this.
	A piggy bank used to save coins by children in some cultures will be considered inappropriate in other cultures.
Language inconsistencies	The English language usage, spellings, as well as pronunciation varies across the world. Any inconsistency in usage is likely to be detrimental to the learning objectives. For instance, the word gas is used for auto fuel in America, instead of the more internationally common word petrol.

Bio-diversity	Animals, plants, and food found across the world vary, and unfamiliar or inconsistent use can be distracting. A lesson on dairy farming will need to take into account the fact that cattle breeds are different across geographies.
Economic realities	Apart from the rich-poor divide, often children from relatively similar socio-economic backgrounds experience different realities. A carpenter in one part of the world may own a car and a house with a lawn, but in a different country, these may be signs of great affluence.

Table 2.1: Diversities that impact learning experience

Do you see why it is important for teachers and instructional designers working on K-12 learning material to analyze the student audience? Analyzing students, their socio-economic realities, and cultural context is helpful to create a detailed profile before you attempt to design a topic, script chapters, or develop lesson plans, as the case may be.

Conclusion

The analysis phase is an attempt to address the *"who"* (audience), *"what"* (content), and *"why"* (learning outcome) for a specific learning context. Through this phase, instructional designers develop a deep understanding of the target learner, which in turn, helps them to use language and apply instructional strategies that are learner centric. For workplace skills and vocational training, the learning outcomes are performance-driven; hence a task/job analysis is also completed. In K-12 and higher education, a government-appointed team completes the analysis, and creates the curriculum. However, instructional designers are still expected to analyze the target audience, so that they design material that suits the learners' context.

In the next chapter, we will address the *Design* phase of the ADDIE model in detail. We will look at how the strengths and limitations of human memory must be considered when we organize topics and chapters to create a program, course, or book outline.

Points to remember

- Analysis is the first stage in the ADDIE model and involves a deep investigation of the three variables, which are, audience, content, and learning outcomes.
- The analysis phase helps us understand and profile the target learner and scope the content and learning outcomes. It enables us to unearth learner

characteristics, which serve as input in scoping the content and identifying instructional strategies. This phase can be completed by using a learner-profiling questionnaire, interviews, and observations.

- For vocational skills and corporate training, a job/task analysis is also completed. The DACUM approach is a popular and time-tested approach to complete this activity.

- The following theories and frameworks help us in understanding the traits of the target learner:
    - *Adult learners:* Andragogy or adult learning principles by Malcolm Knowles
    - *Young students:* William Perry's theory of cognitive and ethical development
    - *School students:* Jean Piaget's theory of cognitive development

- There is no universally accepted pedagogical theory for vocational skills – in the absence of one, a thorough audience analysis helps in understanding the target learner.

Multiple choice questions

1. **The analysis phase involves collecting information on which of the following?**
    a) Learner motivation
    b) Target audience
    c) Learning principles
    d) Working memory

2. **Jean Piaget's theory of cognitive development helps us understand which audience profile?**
    a) Vocational learners
    b) College students
    c) Workplace professionals
    d) School students

3. As per Piaget's stages of cognitive development, when students enter the _____ stage, they gain the ability to think in an abstract manner.

   a) Sensory motor
   b) Pre-operational
   c) Formal operational
   d) Concrete operational

4. Which of these is NOT an adult learning trait?

   a) Seeking immediate feedback and gratification
   b) Interested in learning topics that can be applied to work
   c) Preferring problem-centered learning
   d) Appreciating inclusion in instructional planning

Answers
1. b
2. d
3. c
4. a

Questions

1. Describe the DACUM approach for conducting job/task analysis.
2. Why is the design of material for vocational training challenging?
3. Explain with examples, why instructional strategies should be context and age appropriate.
4. Why should instructional material for workplace skills and vocational training be task-oriented?
5. Describe Piaget's stages of cognitive development among children.

Key terms

- *Multiple Intelligences Theory:* According to this theory proposed by Howard Gardner, humans possess different kinds of intelligence, and one may be more dominant than the others. He identifies eight intelligences, which include words, numbers, pictures, music, social interactions, introspection, physical movement, and appreciating nature.

- *Audience analysis:* This is the formal process of gathering learner traits, needs, and constraints through interviews or surveys.

- *Content analysis:* This is the formal process of scoping the content to address specific learning outcomes.

- *Andragogy:* It is the term given to the principles of adult learning as propounded by Malcolm Knowles.

- *Job analysis:* This is the process of systematically identifying the fundamental elements of a job, and the knowledge and skills required for performing the job efficiently.

- *Curriculum:* This term is used to describe a group of courses that must be successfully completed to earn a certificate/degree from a school or college, or to perform a task efficiently in the workplace.

- *Content outline:* This term is used to refer to the structure of a course or program, which includes the key topics.

- *Problem-centric learning:* When instructional material or the instructional process is designed around a problem or real-world tasks, which learners have to solve actively, it is known as problem-centric learning.

- *Content-centric learning:* When instructional material or the instructional process is designed around theory or concepts, which are explained to learners by teachers and experts, it is known as content-centric learning.

CHAPTER 3
Designing the Outline

Introduction

Danny got a new puzzle and couldn't wait to lay his hands on it. He loved playing with puzzles, and would often time himself when he attempted to complete one, so that he could break his previous record. But since he had his term tests, he kept it aside and decided to work on it later.

After the term test, when Danny went to pick the puzzle, he was in for a shock. The puzzle pieces were strewn all over the floor and the carton that contained it was missing. Looks like his little brother got to it before he could. He carefully picked up the pieces and quickly counted them – thank God, all the 500 pieces were there. But, alas, his little brother had thrown away the carton – which by the way carried the big picture!

Now it was almost impossible for Danny to put together the puzzle – how could he without the carton, which depicted the picture? He couldn't possibly piece together the 500 pieces and get it right unless he referred to the picture for the pattern. The puzzle pieces were now useless to him. Had he, at least, seen the picture a few times, he could have pieced them together from memory – yes, he can do that for most of his older puzzles that he has because the visual is imprinted in his memory.

The starting point in the Design phase of the ADDIE methodology is the creation of an outline – the book or chapter outline, the program outline, or the course outline for a training program. This outline should provide the big picture to the learners. In the face of it, while this may seem like an easy task to accomplish, a lot of careful thought must go into it. It is, after all, the foundation – the building blocks on which other design features will rest. It is the blue print of the course or program that should give the learners a bird's-eye view.

Structure

In this chapter, we will discuss the following topics:

- Working memory
- Cognitive load theory
- Types of cognitive load
- Patterning as a brain function
- Outline design: Considerations

Objectives

After studying this chapter, you will be able to describe the significance of working memory, and its strength and limitations. In addition, you will be able to explain the concept of cognitive load theory and the different types of cognitive load that we face when we learn something. Further, you will be able to understand how patterning is an important function of our brain. Finally, you will be able to apply all these concepts in the design of the table of contents of a book, or a program, or the content outline of a course.

Memory stages

Recall that in *Chapter1, Understanding Instructional Design*, we introduced the constants and variables in instructional design. Then in *Chapter 2, Analyzing Learning Need*, we discussed the three variables, which are the audience, content, and learning outcomes. In this chapter, we will go through one of the constants, **memory**. We will start with how our brain processes information and the strengths and weaknesses of our memory system which must be taken into account when you design an outline.

Figure 3.1 depicts the ADDIE model and the variables and constants that make up the learning ecosystem:

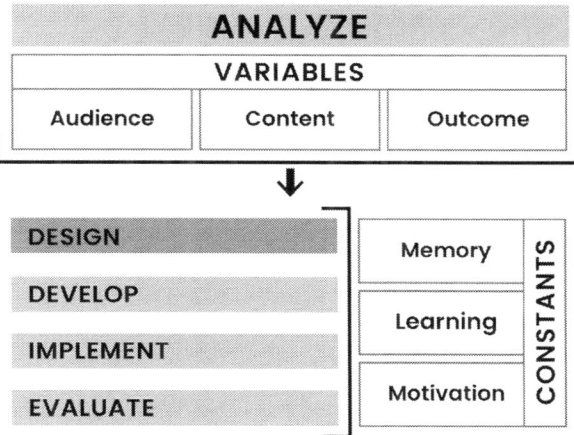

Figure 3.1: ADDIE Model (Adapted version)

The human brain has a limited capacity to process information. It cannot sustain attention on any activity over a period of time. You hear, see, and feel many things, but you can only remember a few. This is because what you feel, hear, or see, goes through various stages of memory. The way memory works is like this – first, you receive new information through your senses; then, you store it temporarily; next, you may rehearse, repeat, or apply this new information, and as a result, it gets stored in your brain permanently. Think of how you learn something before an examination. You read the information many times (sensory), repeat it in your mind or aloud (working), and then it gets stored (long-term).

The first stage is **sensory** memory, which contains receptors that briefly hold on to only that information, which enters through our senses. The second stage is **working** memory, a temporary storage facility. It is also called short-term memory and relates to what we are thinking about at any given point in time. Working memory is used when we perform a task or *learn something new*. As you are reading this now and trying to understand it, your working memory is active. The third stage is **long-term** memory. It provides the lasting retention of information, from minutes to a lifetime. It stores knowledge and a record of prior events, and each one of us will have many such knowledge and records stored in our brain. Since working memory is what aids the learning process, as instructional designers, we must understand its strength and weaknesses well.

Figure 3.2 shows all three stages of memory:

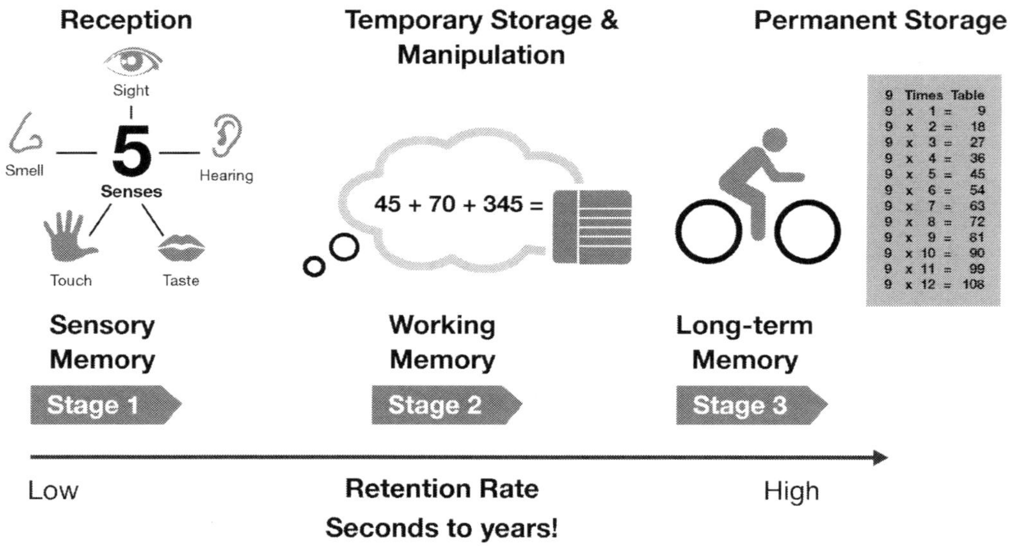

Reception — **Sensory Memory** — Stage 1
Temporary Storage & Manipulation — **Working Memory** — Stage 2
Permanent Storage — **Long-term Memory** — Stage 3

Low ← **Retention Rate** — Seconds to years! → High

Figure 3.2: Memory stages

Working memory

As mentioned earlier, working memory is involved when we are working on a task or solving a problem. Here is a little exercise to help you understand this better. Solve the following mathematical problem mentally – without a calculator, or a paper and pencil.

What is the product of 50 × 50?

You will obviously calculate this quickly in your head, and arrive at the answer. But, what if the numbers were changed and made larger and complex, say something like 45382 × 72651? Most of us will need a paper and pencil (or a calculator) to arrive at the answer. *Table 3.1* displays how the three memory types interplay for completing this task:

What you did	Memory Type	Characteristics
Read the question using your eyes and it registered in your brain.	Sensory Memory	Reception of information through the senses
Held the two numbers (50 and 50) in your brain.	Working Memory	Temporary Storage

| Recalled (brought to mind) the procedure for multiplication. | Long-term Memory | Permanent Storage |
| Multiplied the two numbers. | Working Memory | Manipulation |

Table 3.1: Memory stages

Given that working memory is involved when we learn something new, we need to understand how it functions. Here is one more question for you to answer before you learn more about working memory.

Can you recall the two large numbers that were given for multiplying in the preceding paragraph?

Tip: For this exercise to be meaningful, think hard, and please don't go back to reading the numbers.

Most of us won't be able to recall the numbers. Why so? Well, it's because our working memory has only a *limited capacity*. It is difficult to hold two large numbers in our brain at the same time. Just think about this. When you go grocery shopping, you would perhaps carry a list if you had to buy more than ten items. On the other hand, if you had to buy only 2-3 items, you would most probably hold it in your memory.

Note: Of course another reason for the inability to recall the two large numbers is that you were focused on understanding something else. But even if the page only had the two numbers and no other information, you will find it hard to recall. Unless of course, you memorized it thoroughly.

Not just limited capacity, working memory has some other shortcomings too. It *tires* from use, and is also easily *distracted*. Think about some classes that you attended as a student. Do you recall the times when your thoughts just drifted away from what the teacher was explaining? When did this happen mostly – was it later in the day, or early in the morning? Chances are that it would have been later in the day because your working memory had been taxed all morning trying to learn many new things, and by afternoon it got tired. Consider another situation. You are trying hard to learn something for a test and a neighbour puts on music in loud volume. Would you be able to concentrate with the same intensity as you had been when there was no music? Again, chances are that you would be distracted because your working memory is easily distracted.

> **Note:** A word of caution here. It is important to understand that context matters a lot with regard to memory. It could be possible that some of us will not get distracted easily for various reasons – we could have cultivated the habit of shutting out distractions, or we are learning something that we enjoy so much that nothing distracts us.

Since the working memory has certain limitations, you need to optimize it. This can be achieved in two ways. One, organize and chunk the content in such a manner that the instructional units or the building blocks are neither too lengthy and complex, nor too short and simple. Two, a single glance of the contents should help the learners visualize the big picture.

Cognitive load theory

Closely associated with the principle of working memory is another principle known as **cognitive load**. The concept of cognitive load was introduced by John Sweller who published an article by the same name in the scientific journal, *Cognitive Science* in 1988. The term sounds rather heavy, doesn't it? Well, it's not. Let's use an analogy to understand this heavy-sounding term. To do so, think through the following questions:

- How many vegetable sandwiches can you eat in a single meal?
- What about pizza slices – how many of those can you eat in a single meal?
- Do you think a child will be able to eat the same number of sandwiches as an adult?
- Can you eat an entire cake or a full pie in one meal?
- Do you think an athlete's food intake will be similar to yours?

Hope all these questions on food have not made you hungry! That wasn't the idea. The purpose of these questions was to highlight the fact that there is a limit to how much we can eat, and that our capacity to eat depends upon factors, such as age, exercise regimen, and the type of food. Just like our stomachs have a certain capacity for food intake, it seems our brains too have a certain capacity for information intake. Simply put, the term cognitive load is something that describes this capacity of the brain.

The effort required to process new information by our working memory is known as cognitive load. Two factors impact cognitive load. Some content is inherently complex, and its very nature places a load on our working memory resources. This is known as **intrinsic load**.

> **Note: Cognitive load can vary depending upon the prior knowledge an individual possesses. What novice learners find difficult may be easy for an expert.**

What makes content complex or high in intrinsic load?

High element interactivity makes the content complex. Element in the academic sense is defined as anything that needs to be learned and processed, or is already learned and processed. Element interactivity refers to the logically related elements in the learning material. Since the elements are related, they must be processed simultaneously in the working memory. These elements need to be connected by the learner in order to develop a deep understanding of the subject. Content with a high number of interacting elements tends to be complex and high on cognitive load. As Sweller says,

"Intrinsic cognitive load is the mental work imposed by the basic characteristics of the information."

Suppose you have to solve a mathematical problem, as displayed in *Example 3.1*. In this example, all the numbers are elements. The parenthesis is also an element. In addition, the symbols for basic arithmetic operations, such as addition, multiplication, and division are elements too. This is an example of high element interactivity, and it represents *intrinsic cognitive load*. But, please do note that the purpose of this example is to help you understand the concept of intrinsic load. If the learner is an expert in the subject, the content may not pose a high cognitive load.

Example 3.1: Intrinsic load

Solve the following problem: $4 + 82 \times (30 \div 5) =$

As instructional designers, we should **manage** the intrinsic load by optimally chunking and sequencing the learning material. We shouldn't pack too many complex concepts within a single learning unit, or stretch a simple concept across many units. Please remember that intrinsic load can vary depending upon what you already know about a concept.

The second type of load is imposed because of how information is presented, and it is known as **extraneous load**. The load is imposed due to the manner in which the material is designed and presented. Instructional designers must be extra cautious when they design online or multimedia learning material. You may add background music to a video lesson, or present tough concepts in an interview format to novice learners – in both these situations, the format of the learning material will cause extraneous load. This load must be **minimized**.

Example 3.2: Extraneous load

Suppose a teacher decides to teach a topic by designing it as a game. This strategy is an example of extraneous load because, along with understanding the concept, the learners will also have to remember the rules of the game.

The third type of cognitive load is **germane load**. This load is imposed on processing or understanding the content. Consider this. When you read or hear the word, dog, what all comes to your mind? Living things, animals, wild animals, pets, dog species, and so on, right? Or, if you read the word cow, you may think of farm animals, barns, dairy products, and so on. These structures that your brain creates around a concept is known as a **schema**. In simple terms, **schema** is the term used to describe the concepts stored in your long-term memory as connected pieces of knowledge. For novice learners, those who are new to a subject, the schema is yet to be constructed. For experts on a subject, the schema has more items and a greater number of connections between the items. Which is why, they are able to easily draw upon complex concepts into their working memory.

Let's illustrate this concept with the help of a scenario. Consider that you are teaching a new recruit in your organization the *storyboarding* process in e-learning. The following list is all that you would need to cover:

- Storyboard
- Writing style
- Gagne's events of instruction
- Learning theories
- Instructional design principles
- Objective writing
- Keller's ARCS
- Bloom's taxonomy
- Interactivity
- Feedback
- Multiple choice questions (MCQs)
- Standards
- Formats
- Style guide

This is a content with high element interactivity. Each element further has concepts and sub-concepts embedded within. Furthermore, these elements are also interconnected. But at the moment, for a novice, these are all disparate terms.

The novice will not be able to connect any of these elements. The same content for e-learning professionals who are trained in the storyboarding process, and have also written a couple of storyboards, would appear less daunting, because they have developed a mental schema through learning, practice and retrieval. Schemas are an efficient way to organize interrelated concepts in a meaningful way.

Figure 3.3 depicts the schema of a novice instructional designer; notice that there are no connections between various concepts:

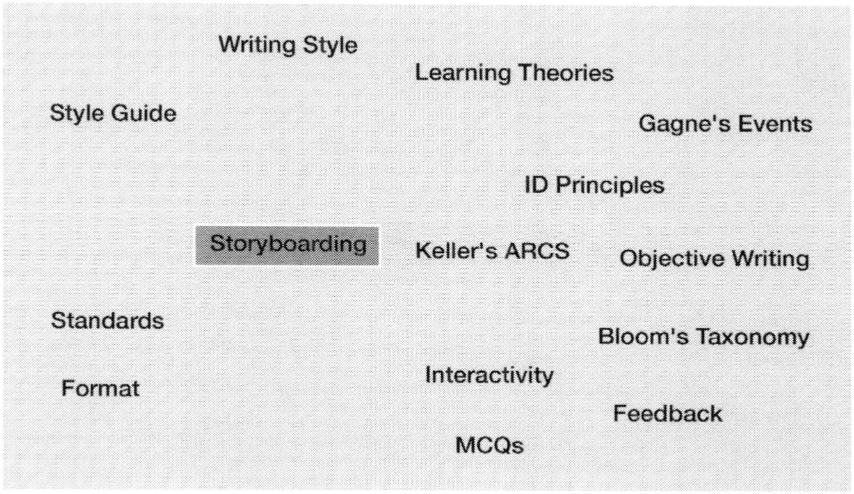

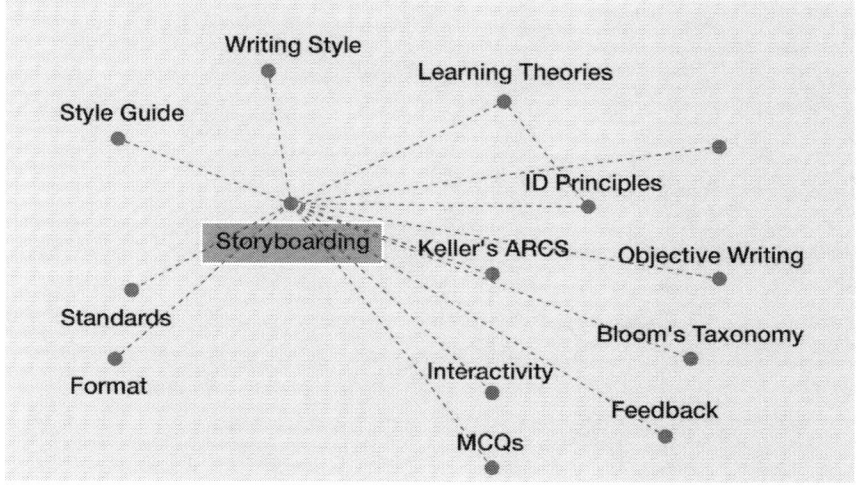

Figure 3.3: Novice schema (storyboarding)

A person with some understanding of the storyboarding process will possess a schema, such as the one shown in *Figure 3.4*:

Figure 3.4: Schema of a professional (storyboarding)

Finally, an e-learning professional with five or more years of experience has learned these concepts and applied it at work many times. Each time the instructional designer wrote a script, the connections between various elements became stronger. The experience also helped the instructional designer to connect more concepts, which perhaps earlier seemed to be unconnected. An expert schema on the scripting process will appear as shown in *Figure 3.5*:

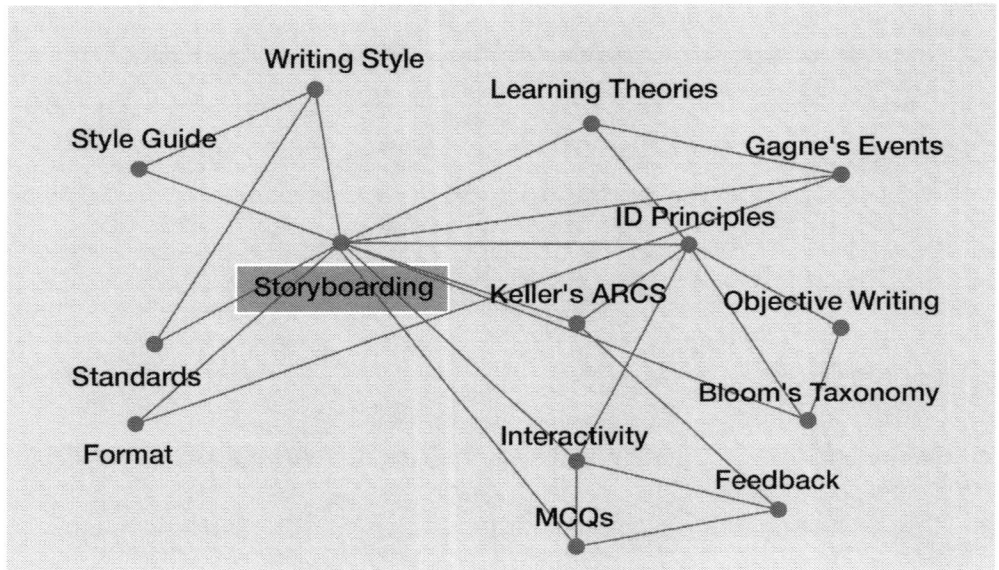

Figure 3.5: Schema of an expert (storyboarding)

Germane load refers to the working memory resources available to learn content with high element interactivity associated with intrinsic cognitive load. As we learned earlier, this type of cognitive load is directly associated with the construction of schema. Teachers, trainers, and instructional designers must try and **maximize** the germane load.

Design implications

Most of those who teach or design learning material will be experts or collaborate with experts in the subject. Being a subject matter expert (SME) is both a strength and a weakness in teaching. The strength is that experts will rarely get the content wrong. However, this could also lead them to unwittingly assume that since the content makes sense to them, it will also make sense to the learner. But, the fact is that it may not, because the learner is new to the subject matter.

Cognitive load theory reminds us that information which is new may overwhelm novice learners, and we should use strategies to present it in a calibrated manner.

For instance, if a textbook chapter is high on intrinsic cognitive load, you can create a *graphic organizer* to help the learners build a schema. Graphic organizers use words and symbols to depict the relationships between various concepts. For example, a fish bone diagram is a graphic organizer that is used to represent the cause-effect relationship. Or if you are designing the outline for an online program with high intrinsic load, you can chunk it in small units and present the content using a pattern that learners can easily relate with.

Table 3.2 summarizes the three types of cognitive load and how you need to handle it to design the outline:

Load	Description	Design Guideline
Intrinsic	Inherent complexity of the content or information.	*Manage* this through chunking.
Extraneous	Elements related to how the information is presented, and which have the potential to overload the learning task.	*Minimize* this – do not add unneccessary elements or elements that will hinder learning .
Germane	It is the memory resources available for understanding the content by creating mental patterns (schema).	*Maximize* this because this load is actually good for learning.

Table 3.2: Types of cognitive load

Patterning

While the working memory and cognitive load theory dealt mostly with the weaknesses of our brain, the patterning principle addresses a unique strength of the human brain. The human brain is always trying to make sense of the environment around us. Our brains process the big picture first and then focus on the details. **Patterns** are our observations organized by the brain into meaningful groups. When we receive new information through one of the senses (sensory memory), it is encoded into patterns (working memory) by our brain before it gets stored or connected to the existing information (long-term memory). Using patterns to present content will help learners to relate new information with what they already know, or help them to encode the new information.

Patterns can be found in all subjects, be it mathematics, science, or languages. It just takes a bit of observation and thinking. For instance, multiplication is a pattern of repeated addition, the Fibonacci sequence is nature's numbering system, while a story adopts the following pattern – exposition, rising action, climax, falling action, and resolution.

Much of what we learn in school is a result of somebody who discovered tacit patterns. For example, Darwin's theory of evolution is based on patterns he observed and put together from the long voyage that he undertook. Heredity principles that we studied in school is because Gregor Mendel carefully observed and recorded the inheritance patterns of pea plant traits.

As instructional designers, we must search for these patterns, and highlight it in the design of the learning material. Teachers and educators should understand this and create learning opportunities that exploits this pattern-recognizing ability of the human brain.

Outline design

While the memory principles impact all learners regardless of age, the manner in which we design the program outlines will vary. For instance, a school-going learner cannot process large amounts of information at once. Hence, we should take this into consideration when we design the structure of a textbook or a lesson plan. Adult learners sign up for a learning program because they want to apply it in the workplace. Therefore, the program outline, which you design for workplace learning must take this into account.

Workplace learning

The final goal of all workplace learning is application. Therefore, before designing the program outline, it is necessary to consult with employees and their supervisors and managers to identify the key tasks that are performed in a certain function, and the knowledge, skills, and attitude needed to accomplish these tasks optimally. As explained in *Chapter 2, Analyzing Learning Needs*, this activity involves audience, task, and needs analysis (DACUM Process). In the design phase, the output from the analysis should be organized, chunked, and sequenced to create the program outline. And, how should that be done? Let's look at two sample program outlines to understand how the memory-related principles we analysed ought to be applied in creating a program outline.

Figure 3.6 displays an outline for a basic course targeted at people who are new to instructional design. The learners are graduates and post-graduates who are looking at making a career in the training industry. After completing this program, they will function as content developers and develop session plans for instructor-led training or create storyboards for simple online learning modules. If you observe the example carefully, you will notice that the outline is content-driven. The topic names reflect the concepts that will be covered in the course.

Critics may argue that people do learn even if the content is not well organized. Some may even argue that making sense from unorganized content will ensure that learning sticks. And that is indeed true. Regardless of whether the content is well organized or not, people still learn because our brains are wired to learn. However, most of us will take a longer time to learn. For novice learners, it is always better to present content in a well-organized form.

Figure 3.6 depicts a sample outline for a beginner's course in instructional design:

Content Outline

1. What is Instructional Design?
2. Guidelines for creating Content Outline
3. Understanding Content Types
4. Learning Outcomes: Bloom's Taxonomy
5. Learning Outcomes: Mager's Format
6. Scripting: Guidelines
7. Scripting: Formats
8. Visuals in Learning: Purpose
9. Visuals in Learning: Types
10. Assessment in Learning: Purpose
11. Assessment in Learning: Types

Figure 3.6: Sample Outline

Let us next look at *Figure 3.7*, which is a reworked version. This one has been created after conducting a thorough *task analysis*, which you learned about in *Chapter 2, Analyzing Learning Needs*. The workflow from the analysis activity is captured, and the tasks have been used to design the program outline. Focus on the topic names in this sample. These topics reflect the key tasks that a content developer will perform to create a single instructional unit. Nested within these topics (tasks) are the concepts and principles. This sample clearly encompasses the three learning principles we looked at previously. The advantage of creating a program outline in this manner is two-fold. One, it provides a clear pattern for the novice learner, so that they can register and store it in the long-term memory. Two, it connects learning with workplace tasks, thereby making the content relevant. This pattern-like approach to the program outline ensures a high recall value. The reworked outline in *Figure 3.7* depicts the key tasks involved in storyboarding as topic/module names:

Discover ID for Beginners: Mind Map

Episode 1- Decoding ID

Episodes	Analysis	Design — Why?	Develop a Topic/Module — Principle/Framework	Implement — Output/Deliverable	Evaluate
2.	Identify Content Type	It helps to define objectives.	Ruth Clark's Content Types	Main Content Type / Secondary Content Types	
3.	Organize Content	It helps to script (ensures flow)	Chunking Rules	Content Flow for the topic	
4.	Specify Objectives	It helps to scope the content / Keep content relevant to meet the topic/module objective	Merrill's Content-Performance Matrix / Mager's Format / Bloom's Taxonomy	Enabling Objectives at Recall/Understand level	
5.	Script the Topic	It ensures that all learning events are included.	Gagne's Events of Instruction	Partial Storyboard / PPT Slide Deck with Content (ILT)	
6.	Visualize the Script	It helps Graphic Designers to get started.	Realistic / Infographic / Metaphor	Partial Storyboard / PPT Slide Deck with Visuals (ILT)	
7.	Create Questions	It helps to evaluate whether learner has understood.	Objective (MCQ, MMCQ, T-F, FIB) / Subjective (Essay, Project)	Production-Ready Storyboard / PPT & Facilitator Guide (ILT)	

Figure 3.7: Reworked Outline

The following are three reasons why the reworked sample is better than the first one:

- **Firstly**, organizing and chunking frees up our working memory and helps us *interact* with the information – see patterns and associations that one would otherwise miss.

- **Secondly**, learning does stick if we struggle with information and structure, it ourselves, but with novice learners, this process takes a lot of time, and some of them may get overwhelmed and anxious.

- **Finally**, the first sample is how most SMEs will design a program outline – it is content driven. They understand their subject so well that they function like Wikipedia; they link a concept with another concept and their knowledge is almost like a web of information. However, if the same is disseminated to novice learners, they could get frustrated. On the other hand, instructional designers are novices in the subject matter. The strategies they adopt will be more learner-centric, which will work better with the learners.

Higher education

The key purpose of higher education is to prepare the students for a career. Therefore, any program outline for higher education must include concepts coupled with a generous dose of practical application. And this ought to reflect in both the prescribed curriculum outline as well as the academic books designed for higher education. As we read in *Chapter 2, Analyzing Learning Need* in the higher education space too, curriculum is designed by a team comprising domain experts, professors, and industry representatives. The selection of content has input from industry, government, community, as well as educators.

Curriculum outline is the blueprint of how and when the concepts will be covered in conjunction with various learning events and activities, such as lectures, discussions, tutorials, lab work, and project or field work. A typical curriculum outline for higher education will include the following:

- The structure and content of the entire program
- The structure and content of each unit (subject) in the program
- The students' experience of learning through varied approaches, such as classroom sessions, online modules, projects, and lab or field work.

Conventional higher education curriculum is mostly classroom based with focus on knowledge of a subject area determined by SMEs. At the advanced level, students may be given the freedom to select their choice of subjects. At the end of the program, the student must clear an examination, a large percentage of which assesses knowledge and understanding related to the subject matter.

Publishers of textbooks and developers of multimedia material are expected to follow the university or institution curriculum while developing instructional material. Common organizing strategies in the design of such material include, but are not limited to, the ones shown in *Table 3.3*:

Strategy	Description
Simple to Complex	Most content is presented in this way. This involves organizing the units of content in sequential chunks beginning with the simple, basic, fundamental concepts and then moving on to describing the more complex and technical concepts.
Chronological	This strategy is used to address the development of a product or concept over a period. For example, when discussing the history of the Internet or the evolution of microcomputers, this strategy is used.
General to Specific	The explanation of concepts and information can also flow from general to specific. This sequence can be reversed too. For instance, one can start with a specific case/instance/example, and then go ahead and give the overall perspective.

Table 3.3: Content organizing strategies

One of the best ways to address practical application of concepts in textbooks is through the inclusion of case studies. A case study is a substantial problem based on a real-life example, or a fictitious one. Case studies provide students an opportunity to investigate a phenomenon within its real-life context through research and empirical inquiry. Textbooks may be designed to include one overarching case study that ties all the concepts together, or several case studies, each of which addresses a single concept or principle. Instructional designers creating material for higher education must collaborate with SMEs to design case studies.

Vocational skills

To design the curriculum or program outline for vocational skills, you will need to identify the knowledge and skills required to perform various tasks that have been identified for a certain job role. To do this, you must understand the difference between declarative and procedural knowledge.

Declarative knowledge in the context of **vocational training** is the knowledge about work-relevant information and tasks. For instance, a cab driver needs to know the following – traffic rules, a basic knowledge of primary and secondary car controls, and the complexities of driving. All this is declarative knowledge. In addition, the cab driver must be able to drive and maintain his/her vehicle. These are procedural knowledge. In short, declarative knowledge refers to the theoretical part that needs to be known and/or understood to accomplish a task. Procedural knowledge addresses how to do something, or how to perform a task. It is the ability to work or produce a tangible work output.

Declarative and procedural knowledge

Let us compare declarative and procedural knowledge, as shown in *Table 3.4*:

	Declarative	**Procedural**
Definition	Knowledge about work-relevant information and tasks	The ability to carry out work-related tasks
Description	• You can only recall and/or understand • Manifests as facts, concepts, and principles • Is assessed through a written exam or viva	• It is the performance of tangible or visible work • It is the performance of cognitive/behavioural work that results in some tangible work output • It is assessed through a project or practical application
Examples	• An organization's revenue goal for a financial year • The best type of manufacturing equipment • The type of training workers need to execute their jobs	• Managing a project • Writing a report • Calculating the maximum load for a truck • Attaching doors to a vehicle in an assembly line

Table 3.4: Declarative versus procedural knowledge

By identifying these categories, you will be able to demarcate the knowledge and skills required for a job role.

For **declarative knowledge**, if the content is simple, then you can address two to four concepts within a module. But, if the content is complex, you may want to address a single concept in a module and include a few examples and exercises within the module, so that the learner acquires mastery over these before proceeding to a new concept in the next module.

For **procedural knowledge** too, if mastering a specific skill requires a lot of practice, then address only a single skill within a module. But do remember that many tasks require coordinated skills (many skills to be performed simultaneously), so do include a module that provides learners the big picture and the opportunity to put/practice all skills in a coordinated way.

Figure 3.8 depicts an example of the program outline from a vocational program for cab drivers presented using a graphic organizer; the unit names are task-based and every unit addresses both declarative and procedural knowledge:

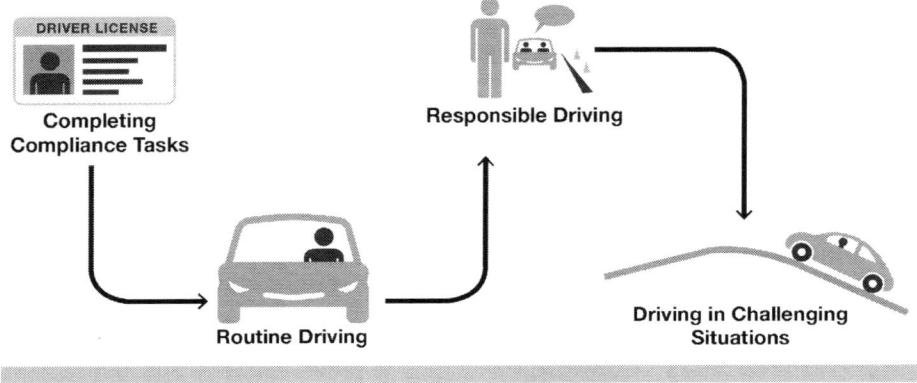

Figure 3.8: *Course outline for cab drivers*

K-12 curriculum

Conventional K-12 curriculum is also mostly classroom based with focus on knowledge of the given subject area determined by subject experts. Therefore, the curriculum or course outline is content-driven and obviously not task-driven. Most often, the curriculum for K-12 is designed by a curriculum team with expertise in developmental and cognitive psychology. Publishers of textbooks and developers of multimedia material are expected to follow the national or state-level curriculum.

Research has shown that the working memory capacity of children increases with age. This implies that children in the primary grade have a smaller working memory capacity as compared to students in the middle and secondary grades. Therefore, the curriculum in primary classes is less intensive than the curriculum in middle and secondary classes. Content is typically organized in a simple to complex sequence. This involves arranging the units of content in sequential chunks beginning with the simple, basic, fundamental concepts and then moving on to describing the more complex and technical concepts.

Conclusion

The outline for a course, program, or a book is the first work output of the design phase in the ADDIE methodology. This output is like the blueprint of the detailed instructional material. The blueprint must be effective to ensure that the rest of the material is too. To create an effective outline, you must understand how our brain works, the limitations of our working memory, and the patterning ability of our brain. We often learn, not the literal things in front of us, but the relations between them. So, when we create an outline, the most important thing that we must do is connect all the concepts and sub-concepts to create the *big picture*. If the outline is well-organized and chunked, it is easier on the working memory, and the learning becomes simpler.

A **program outline** is a useful tool for instructional designers to scope the content to be addressed. It helps the learner to see the big picture, and the instructional designer to stick to teaching what is necessary to meet the learning outcomes.

Another task needs to be accomplished in tandem with the creation of an outline. This task involves specifying the learning outcomes.

In the next chapter, we will look at how the learning outcomes must be written and learn about some popular formats for completing this task.

Points to remember

- The program outline, course outline, or curriculum is the blueprint of the course or program. It is the basic foundation on which the entire course or program will rest. Therefore, it should provide the big picture to the learners.

- Working memory is what we use when we learn something new. Understanding its strength and limitations helps us design the outlines that are organized to optimize the strengths and tide over the limitations.

- The patterning strength of the working memory must be optimized when you create a program outline. This can be done through the use of graphic organizers, which will serve as a mental model for the learners.

- There are three types of cognitive load. We must manage the intrinsic load, minimize the extraneous load, and maximize the germane load.

- While the program outline lays down the basic structure and flow of a course or program, do not treat it as a menu or a list of topics. It should be designed in such a way that the entire course can be anchored in it. This will provide the learners with the big picture and enable them to recall the concepts through association.

Multiple choice questions

1. **Which of the following is NOT a working memory limitation?**
    a) Tires from use
    b) Can't process information

c) Is limited in capacity

d) Is easily distracted

2. **Assuming that we are considering novice learners, which of the following concepts will have the highest intrinsic cognitive load?**

   a) Supplementary angles

   b) Causes for World War II

   c) Factors influencing seasons

   d) Concept of democracy

3. **Which one of the following cognitive loads should be maximized?**

   a) Intrinsic

   b) Germane

   c) Extraneous

4. **If some content is high in cognitive load, what should you NOT do?**

   a) Identify patterns

   b) Create a graphic organizer

   c) Design small units

   d) Increase extraneous load

Answers

1. b
2. a
3. b
4. d

Questions

1. What are the three types of cognitive load and how should you handle each? Explain with examples.

2. Define the concept of element interactivity.

3. Distinguish between procedural and declarative knowledge.

4. Explain how the design of the outline for workplace learning and vocational skills differ from the outline for K-12 and higher education.

Key terms

- *Sensory memory*: It is the first stage of memory that briefly holds on to only that information which enters through our senses.

- *Working memory*: It is the second stage of memory, which is a temporary storage facility, and is used when we perform a task or learn something new.

- *Long-term memory*: This is the third stage of memory, which provides the lasting retention of information, from minutes to a lifetime.

- *Cognitive load:* It is the effort required to process new information by our working memory.

- *Element interactivity*: This term is used to describe the logically related elements in the learning material.

- *Intrinsic load*: It is the load imposed by the content due to high element interactivity.

- *Extraneous load*: It is the load created by elements related to how the information is presented, and which have the potential to overload the learning task.

- *Schema*: These are structures that your brain creates around a concept.

- *Germane load*: It is the memory resources available for understanding the content by creating mental patterns (schema).

- *Graphic organizers*: These are words and symbols organized visually to depict the relationships between various concepts.

- *Patterns*: These are the observations of our environment organized by the brain into meaningful groups.

- *Module:* In the learning context, a module is a single unit of content presented to address a specific learning outcome.

- *Storyboarding*: It is the process of organizing content and detailing it with examples for an e-learning module.

CHAPTER 4
Defining Learning Outcomes

Introduction

Lewis Carroll's book, *Alice's Adventures in Wonderland* is fascinating in different ways to different people. Many find it so because it gives numerous philosophical and psychological insights. There are a few conversations in the book that are loaded with meaning, and this one between Alice and the Mock Turtle is no different.

> *Mock Turtle:* They were obliged to have him with them! No wise fish would go anywhere without a porpoise"!
>
> *Alice:* "Wouldn't it really"?
>
> *Mock Turtle:* "Of course not. Why, if a fish came to me, and told me he was going on a journey, I should say "With what porpoise?"
>
> *Alice:* Don't you mean "purpose"?

Though the Mock Turtle uses the word "porpoise", which means a small-toothed whale, litterateurs say that the word porpoise here is an intended pun for the word, *purpose*. The author used this word by design to convey the message that every journey should have a purpose, a goal.

What about learning then? Isn't that also a journey in many ways? When we embark on a journey, we select a destination to arrive at, and based on that, we decide the best route and the mode of transport. Similarly, defining the learning outcomes is necessary before we develop the instructional plan and instructional materials. Think about this – if we don't have a specific learning outcome, how will we put together the instructional material? And, how will we know on what concepts to assess our learners? Last, but not the least, how will we determine whether our instructional material has helped the learners to learn?

So, you see, if we do not specify what the learners' need to achieve at the end of a course or program, what we create would be no different from a search engine on the Internet.

Structure

In this chapter, we will discuss the following topics:

- Significance of learning outcomes
- Mager's format for writing learning outcomes
- Domains of learning: cognitive, affective, and psychomotor
- Bloom's taxonomy of the cognitive domain
- Learning outcomes for K-12, higher education, vocational skills, and workplace training

Objectives

After studying this chapter, you will be able to describe the significance of the learning outcomes. In addition, you will be able to explain the frameworks that help us define the learning outcomes. Further, you will be able to analyze the strengths and shortcomings of these frameworks. And finally, you will be able to apply the frameworks judiciously to define the learning outcomes at the course, program, session, and chapter or module levels.

Different terminologies

As you can see in *Figure 4.1*, **outcome** is one of the three variables in any instructional context. In this chapter, we will be addressing this variable in detail. Defining the learning outcomes is part of the Design phase in the ADDIE model. And to complete this activity, there are some established frameworks which can be used. We will also explore these frameworks, and illustrate how they help us define the learning outcomes.

Figure 4.1 displays the ADDIE model with the learning variables and constants:

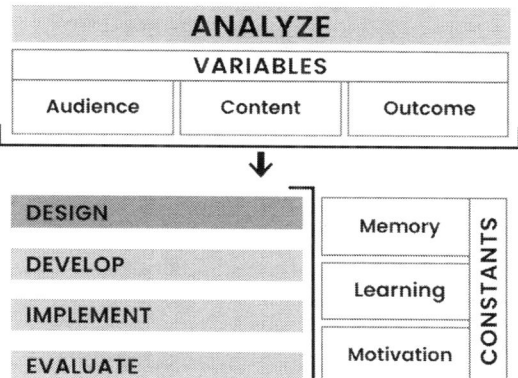

Figure 4.1: ADDIE Model (Adapted version)

To understand the concept of learning outcomes, let us get a small hurdle out of the way. Every profession has a unique vocabulary. Peruse a few marketing papers and you will see a few weasel words that are used as hyperbole. Go through some technical articles, and you will find yourself in a maze of technical jargon. In the learning domain, academics and practitioners revel in assigning different nomenclatures to the same concept – aim, goal, outcome – objectives being the case in point. Let us first try and put these terms in perspective.

Learning outcomes specify what a typical learner will have achieved at the end of a course, a session, or a class. The terms *curriculum* or *program goals*, and *aim* imply long-term targets, while *learning outcomes* and *learning objectives* imply short-term ones. *Learning objective* is used from the instructor's perspective, and on the other hand, *learning outcome i*s stated from the learner's perspective. We will use the term *learning outcome* throughout this book.

Figure 4.2 depicts the concept of learning outcomes from both the instructor's and the learner's perspectives:

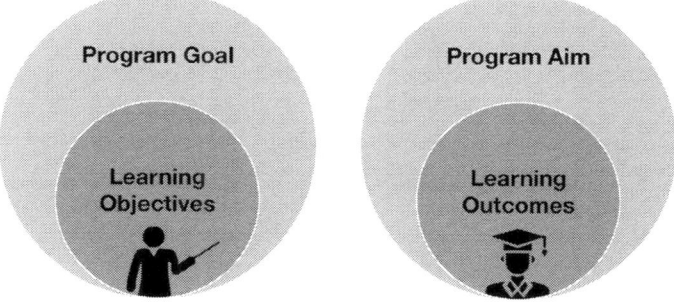

Figure 4.2: Learning outcomes from instructor and learner perspectives

Purpose of learning outcomes

Let us start with a basic question – why do we learn? Simply put, there are three basic reasons for learning anything – to gain *knowledge* and *understanding*, to acquire some *skill*, or to develop certain *attitudes*.

For instance, a K-12 teacher is expected to know and understand subject-specific concepts and principles, as well as pedagogical principles – this is *knowledge*. The teacher is required to maintain basic information about her students through computers connected to the school's network, manage the classroom, and work with other teachers – these are *skills, such as computer skills, typing skills, and teamwork skills*. Last, but not the least, she is expected to keep abreast of the changes happening in the profession, proactively respond to these changes, and take the initiative to upskill herself – this is *attitude*.

Learning outcomes help in communicating with the learners, the change that will take place in their knowledge, skills, and attitude, as a result of going through an instructional intervention.

But as we discussed earlier, learning outcomes are not meant only for the learners. They are of great significance to teachers and instructional designers too. By defining the learning outcomes, they can scope the content, identify learning strategies, and design relevant interactions and assessments.

Table 4.1 summarizes the purpose of learning outcomes for learners and instructional designers:

Purpose: For the learner	Purpose: For the teacher, trainer, or instructional designer
• Know what exactly the learners need to remember/recall. • Know what exactly the learners will do (what tasks they will perform) in real situations. • Understand the behaviors expected from them.	• Scope the content • Identify appropriate learning strategies • Design relevant interactions and assessments.

Table 4.1: Purpose of Learning Outcomes

Frameworks for learning outcomes

When you get down to writing learning outcomes, there are two factors to consider– one, *how* to write learning outcomes, and two, *what* the learning outcomes must address. The former deals with the *lexicon*, that is the choice of words, and the latter, the *semantics* or *the intent*.

Figure 4.3 captures these two factors to be considered, and the names of the educationists, who designed the frameworks to address these:

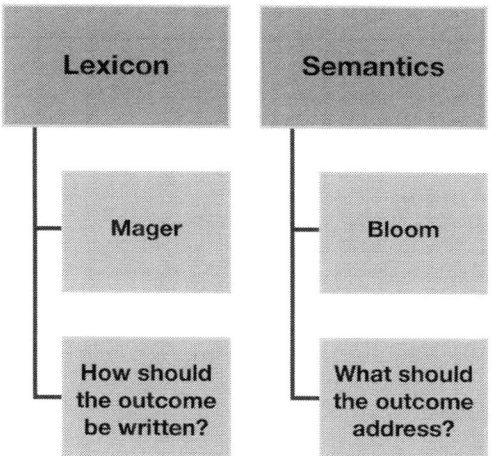

Figure 4.3: *Considerations for writing learning outcomes*

Let's look at the *lexicon* or the *how* factor first.

Mager's format

In 1975, Robert Mager came up with the format for writing learning outcomes. He referred to it as behavioral objectives, and not learning outcomes. This format is widely used in the teaching and training sector. As proposed by Mager, a well-written behavioral objective has the following three parts:

- **Performance**: What the learner will be able to do after the instruction
- **Condition**: The situation under which the performance will be assessed
- **Criteria**: The standards for measuring the performance

The following is an example of a learning outcome written using Mager's format:

Example 4.1: Learning outcome as per Mager's format

Learning Outcome: Create a document with tables and images in MS Word with no formatting or spelling errors.

Performance: Create a document in MS Word

Condition: With tables and images

Criteria: No formatting or spelling errors

The following is another example of a learning outcome written using the same format:

Example 4.2: Learning outcome as per Mager's format

Learning Outcome: Given the cost price and discount percentage, accurately calculate the total savings.

Performance: Calculate total savings

Condition: Given the cost price and discount percentage

Criteria: Accurately

While, in theory, this makes for a great case, in practice, including the condition and criterion in the learning outcomes makes them long-winded and verbose. Hence, the criterion component is rarely included in outcome statements while the condition component is included when there is more than one way to accomplish a task, and only one of these is to be learned.

Of the three components, great emphasis is placed on the *performance* part, which must be written using specific measurable verbs. According to Mager, these verbs are important as they help to clearly measure the success or failure of the learner in completing a learning task. He recommended that verbs such as *know* and *understand* be avoided because these are ambiguous and not clearly measurable.

> **Note: Using words such as know and understand is acceptable in the education domain. Norman Gronlund, an author of many books on teaching, proposes the use of these words in learning outcomes, if they are followed by specific verbs, such as list, identify etc. However, his approach doesn't involve specifying condition and criteria.**

Bloom's taxonomy

Let's now move on to the second factor, which is the "semantics" or the "what" of writing learning outcomes. To do so, let us revisit the three reasons for learning something, which was addressed earlier in this chapter, using the example of a teacher. Recall that we had discussed how the teacher needs to have some *knowledge*, certain *skills,* and a certain *attitude*. Again, as stated earlier, a drawback in academic writing is that a *rose is called by many other names!* In workplace and vocational training, knowledge and skills may collectively be referred to as *domain skills* or *technical skills*, and attitude as *soft skills,* while academics have a different nomenclature for these, which are as follows:

- **Knowledge**: *Cognitive Domain*, the capacity to think or the intellectual skills
- **Skills**: *Psychomotor Domain*, the capacity to apply physical skills
- **Attitude**: *Affective Domain*, the capacity to value, appreciate, and care

Table 4.2 captures the various domains and the terms used to describe these in the education and training sectors:

Area	Education	Training
Knowledge	Cognitive domain	Knowledge
Skills	Psychomotor domain	Technical or domain skills
Attitude	Affective domain	Soft skills

Table 4.2: Learning Domains

These three domains, cognitive, affective, and psychomotor, were first introduced to the world in 1948, when a group of educators undertook the task of classifying education goals and objectives. Work on the cognitive domain was completed in the 1950s and is commonly referred to as *Bloom's taxonomy of the Cognitive Domain* (Bloom, Englehart, Furst, Hill, and Krathwohl, 1956). This taxonomy progresses from the most basic to the most advanced levels.

The six levels in the cognitive domain are displayed in *Table 4.3*:

Level	Description	Specific skills
Knowledge	Learner recalls or retrieves previously learned information.	Knowledge of: • Specifics • Techniques of dealing with specifics • Universals and abstractions
Comprehension	Learner comprehends the meaning, translation, interpolation, and interpretation of instructions and problems.	Ability to: • Translate • Interpret • Extrapolate
Application	Learner uses a concept in a new situation or uses an abstraction in concrete situations.	Ability to use abstractions in general situations

Level	Description	Specific skills
Analysis	Learner separates material or concepts into component parts so that its organizational structure may be understood.	Ability to analyze: • Elements • Relationships • Organizational principles
Evaluation	Learner makes judgments about the value of ideas or materials.	Ability to judge based on: • Internal evidence • External evidence
Synthesis	Learner builds a structure or pattern from diverse elements; puts parts together to form a new whole.	Ability to produce: • Unique communication • Unique plan/proposal • Abstract set of relations

Table 4.3: Bloom's taxonomy of the Cognitive Domain

The following is an example of Bloom levels for a workshop in fiction-writing:

Example 4.3:

- **Knowledge**: List the elements of a story OR identify different genres in fiction-writing.
- **Comprehension**: Illustrate the various literary genres using examples from popular fiction.
- **Application**: Write a short story in the romantic genre.
- **Analysis**: Analyze the book, Battle Hymn of the Tiger Mother, by Amy Chua and prepare a report describing if it is fiction or non-fiction.
- **Evaluation**: Review the book, The Curious Incident of the Dog in the Night-time by Mark Haddon.
- **Synthesis**: Write a short story by mixing two genres.

Note: Example 4.3 is meant to help you differentiate between the various Bloom levels. In the real world, as you try to apply this to a different subject or area, you may not be able to identify all the levels, and/or differentiate between the levels because the levels are not watertight. Some instructional designers may differ on the levels even in this example. This is one of the drawbacks in Bloom's taxonomy.

Bloom's taxonomy is a widely used framework for specifying the learning outcomes for mental and intellectual skills. It also offers a list of verbs for each of the six levels. Over a period, especially with the proliferation of the Internet, this list of verbs has been widely circulated and blindly used. It seems Benjamin Bloom, was not off the mark when he stated the following in the book, *The Taxonomy of Educational Objectives*:

> *"There was some concern expressed in the early meetings that the availability of the taxonomy might tend to abort the thinking and planning of teachers with regard to curriculum, particularly if teachers merely selected what they believed to be desirable objectives from the list provided in the taxonomy."*

In current times, one sees many teachers and instructional designers resorting to pick a verb from the list as given by Bloom and his co-authors. To understand why this mistake is made, you must understand the difference between the *descriptive* and *prescriptive* frameworks.

Descriptive versus prescriptive frameworks

Descriptive frameworks explain how things are, or how things work. On the other hand, **prescriptive frameworks** provide a template or a recommended procedure. **Bloom's taxonomy** is an attempt to structure the process of thinking from simple to complex – it describes how thinking is structured in human brains, or how thinking works. In that sense, it is a descriptive framework and a unique contribution to education. But attempting to use it as a prescriptive framework can do more harm than good to the design of instructional materials.

Rather than trying to map learning outcomes to a certain level of Bloom's taxonomy, understanding it as a descriptive framework that attempts to structure the thinking process will help us design the instructional material in such a manner that it addresses both simple and complex cognitive tasks.

Critiquing Bloom's taxonomy

Bloom's taxonomy, though widely used, is criticized by academics for not being founded upon sound research and brain science. Critics argue that thinking isn't such a linear process and may not necessarily evolve through these stages sequentially. Also, higher-order thinking does not depend upon mastering the lower levels. Even the order of levels is debatable. For example, you may analyze information to understand it. Then, how can *analyze* be at a higher level than *understand*?

The framework is also criticized because there is little consensus between designers and educators regarding the levels. Given any learning outcome, it might be classified into either of the two lowest levels (knowledge or comprehension) or into any of the four highest levels (application, analysis, synthesis, and evaluation) by different designers.

So, how can we use Bloom's taxonomy optimally? One way to do so is to exploit the strengths of the framework and understand its inherent weaknesses.

Figure 4.4 captures the strengths (S) and weaknesses (W) of the framework, and the corresponding opportunities (O) and threats (T) of Bloom's taxonomy:

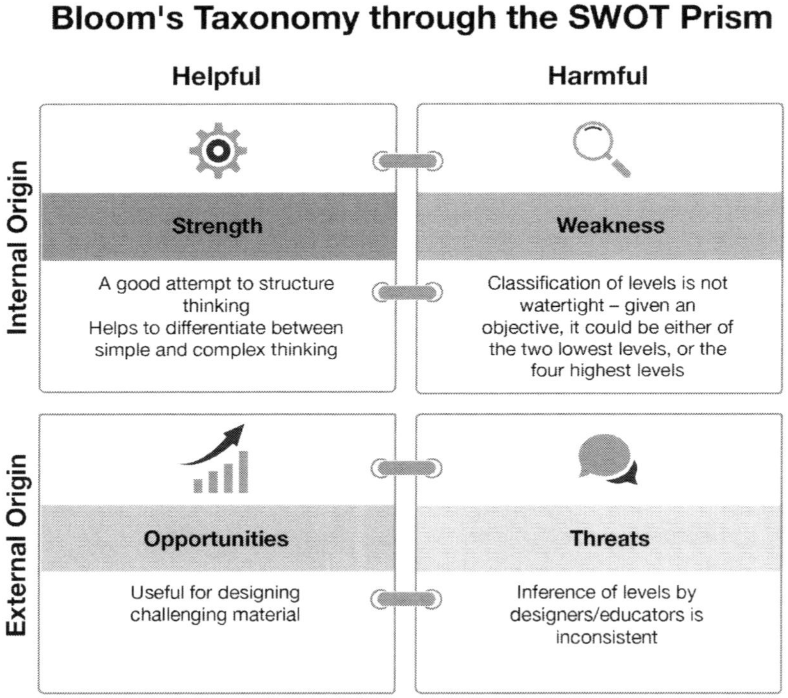

Bloom's Taxonomy through the SWOT Prism

	Helpful	Harmful
Internal Origin	**Strength** A good attempt to structure thinking Helps to differentiate between simple and complex thinking	**Weakness** Classification of levels is not watertight – given an objective, it could be either of the two lowest levels, or the four highest levels
External Origin	**Opportunities** Useful for designing challenging material	**Threats** Inference of levels by designers/educators is inconsistent

Figure 4.4: Bloom's Taxonomy through the SWOT prism

So, is there a workaround to Bloom's taxonomy, and if there is, what is it? Let's see.

A workaround to Bloom's taxonomy

The aim of any learning must be to use it in some form in the real world. It either serves as background information essential for a person to complete a task, or it may manifest in the performance of the task itself. Remember, the concepts of declarative and procedural knowledge that we addressed in *Chapter 3, Designing the Outline*. You would recall that the former implies knowledge of work-relevant information, and the latter is the ability to complete the tasks. When we consider the learning outcomes, this directly translates into two levels – *knowing* information (declarative) and *applying* information (procedural).

You may have a training program that is meant to address only the *recall* of concepts for valid reasons, such as *compliance rules* in the workplace, or *Newton's laws of motion* for school students. In such situations, the learning outcome can be *recall/understand*. But these outcomes must serve only as enablers for a larger outcome/goal – to use it in real life or to identify the manifestations of these in the real world around us.

> **Tip: Apply is misunderstood by many to mean solving computational problems in mathematics or completing observable tasks, such as a nurse administering an injection. However, in topics that are purely theoretical, identifying manifestations (examples) is a form of application too.**

We can surmise that there are two levels in learning – you either *recall/understand* (declarative) it or you *apply/use* (procedural) it. It is better to work with these two clear levels rather than the six levels in Bloom's taxonomy, which are separated by fuzzy distinctions. The following is an example of declarative and procedural learning outcomes in education:

Example 4.4: Learning outcomes in education

- **Recall/Understand**: Describe Newton's laws of motion.
- **Apply/Use**: Given the situations, identify which of the Newton's laws of motion it demonstrates.

The following is an example of declarative and procedural learning outcomes in training:

Example 4.5: Learning outcomes in training

- **Recall/Understand**: Describe the six levels in Bloom's taxonomy
- **Apply/Use**: Write the learning outcomes mapping to Bloom levels 2 and 3 for a given context.

Writing learning outcomes

Writing learning outcomes is part of the instructional planning process, and this task is completed in the Design phase of the ADDIE model. Recall the following two points that were addressed earlier:

i. In *Chapter 1, Understanding Instructional Design*, we saw that the student, program, and institution goals are laid down by a committee of experts for higher education and vocational skills. In the same chapter, we also saw that for K-12, the grade-level outcomes and course goals are specified by a similar committee.

ii. Now, recall the difference between program aim/goal and learning outcomes that we addressed earlier in the chapter, and which is represented through *Figure 4.2*.

From points (i) and (ii), we can conclude that for higher education, vocational training and K-12, the program aim/goal is already specified, and teachers and instructional designers must define the learning outcomes at the next level, such as chapter, topic, or session.

On the other hand, for workplace learning, instructional designers will also have to define the program or course goal, which they will do so in collaboration with **subject matter experts (SMEs)**.

Outcomes for workplace learning

It is rare in the working world to learn something purely for the sake of knowledge. Ultimately everything that one knows must be put to use in some form or the other. As instructional designers, you may learn about Bloom's taxonomy, but the purpose of this is not to recall the levels; rather it is to use the framework in designing the learning material that helps develop thinking skills. In short, knowledge gained must translate to actions in the workplace.

Developing attitudes or soft skills are also a great focus in workplace learning, especially in the modern-day corporate setups. Skills in leadership, teamwork, ethics, communication, conflict resolution, and so on are mandatory to succeed in today's workplace.

Psychomotor skills are important in many trades and professional fields, including engineering and technology and science and healthcare. In most cases, employees would possess these skills at entry-level because they hold a professional qualification. However, at times, there may be focus on these skills in workplace training, to serve as refresher training or if some new equipment has been introduced. The following is an example of the learning outcomes at the *recall/understand* levels in the workplace:

Example 4.6: An orientation module on leadership for new managers

Recall/Understand(Declarative knowledge)

- Describe various leadership theories.
- Explain how to lead with integrity.
- Identify techniques to groom high-performing employees.

Apply/Use (Procedural knowledge: Soft Skills)

- Assist the team members to develop and increase their self-awareness, so that they understand their own strengths and weakness.

- Apply ethical perspectives to ethical situations.
- Apply relevant techniques to groom high-performing employees.

The following is an example of the outcomes at the *apply/use* levels in workplace scenarios:

Example 4.7: An orientation module on refrigeration and air conditioning for new engineers

Recall/Understand (Declarative knowledge)

- Illustrate safety standards and technical developments in the industry.
- Identify the tools, materials, and equipment used in the trade.

Apply/Use (Procedural knowledge: Technical Skills)

- Safely perform routine tasks to maintain air-conditioners and chillers in a cold-storage facility.
- Demonstrate the correct use of tools, materials, and equipment used in the trade.

Outcomes in higher education

As explained in *Chapter 3, Designing the Outline*, the most important goal of higher education is to prepare the students for a career. While this calls for mastery of concepts and principles in the chosen field (*domain knowledge and skills*), it also requires that students to cultivate other skills and attitude (*soft skills*) that will serve them to function effectively in the workplace. The proportion and types of learning outcomes will depend upon the nature of the profession. For programs that are purely academic in nature, the focus would obviously be on mastering the domain from a cognitive perspective, which is to develop intellectual skills. Refer to the following example:

Example 4.8: A graduate course in Economics, for the topic, Introduction to Free Market Economy

Recall/Understand (Declarative knowledge)

- Define the terms demand and supply.
- Describe the factors that impact the demand of a commodity.

Apply/Use (Procedural knowledge: Cognitive Skills)

- Determine the impact of inflation on the demand of a commodity in a given scenario.

Outcomes for vocational training

For vocational training programs, there should be a good mix of all three types of outcomes – *cognitive, affective,* and *psychomotor*. Depending upon the vocation, one of these domains will have a wider and deeper coverage. For instance, in the **Information Technology Enabled Service (ITES)** sector, training in cognitive and affective domains may be necessary, but both are equally important. On the other hand, for the carpentry sector, training in psychomotor and cognitive domains may be required, but the psychomotor domain may be more significant.

Figure 4.5 depicts how the training outcomes may vary across different domains:

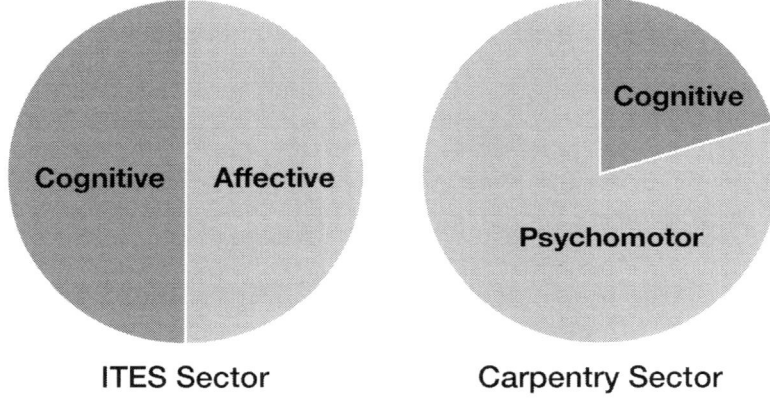

Figure 4.5: Possible skill division in two different sectors

The significance of a domain will also increase or decrease depending upon the level for which the training is being designed. For instance, senior people with experience in most vocations will be taking up leadership positions that involve people management. Therefore, suppose you are designing training material for senior levels in the ITES sector, then you may need to focus on the affective domain more than the cognitive domain.

Figure 4.6 depicts how the training outcomes may vary based on experience of the target audience:

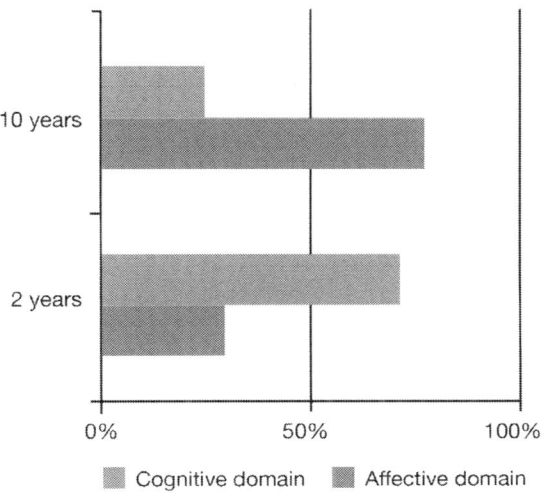

Figure 4.6: Possible skill division depending upon years of experience

The following example showcases the outcomes for an introductory course in nursing:

Example 4.9: An introductory course in nursing

Recall/Understand (Declarative knowledge)

- Describe the nursing process – Assessment, Diagnosis, Planning, Implementation, and Evaluation (ADPIE)
- Identify the various patient-handling equipment and their functions

Apply/Use (Procedural knowledge: Soft Skills)

- Use the nursing process as a purposeful and goal-directed guideline for quality, individually-centered care

Apply/Use (Procedural knowledge: Psychomotor Skills)

- Utilize the patient handling equipment
- Administer medicines intravenously
- Insert and remove catheter

Outcomes in K-12

The purpose of school education is the all-round development of a child, and to produce productive and responsible citizens equipped with the essential competencies and skills for both life-long learning and employment. The overarching purpose is to create workers who have skills to fill and perform the available jobs. At the same time, schools seek to develop active citizens, helping children develop their own capacity for personal achievement and for contributing to the society as active citizens in a democracy. This implies that the learning outcomes for K-12 should be a judicious mix of cognitive, affective, and psychomotor domains.

The following example depicts the sample learning outcomes from an introductory course on computers for K-12:

Example 4.10: An introductory course on computers for middle school students

Cognitive domain

- Describe the advantages of computer
- Complete basic tasks, such as creating a Time Table in MS Word.

Affective domain

- Appreciate how computers help us in becoming more efficient and productive.

Psychomotor domain

- Use computer peripherals, such as keyboard and mouse.

The following is an example of the learning outcomes related to language learning in K-12:

Example 4.11: Language for primary grades

Cognitive domain

- Develop a vocabulary– recall words relevant to the age group/grade
- Ask and answer questions using basic vocabulary
- Respond and converse in simple English

Psychomotor domain

- Speak clearly
- Communicate to be understood

Affective domain

- Develop the habit of reading for information and pleasure
- Develop sensitivity towards one's culture and heritage, and aspects of contemporary life and languages

Conclusion

In this chapter, we addressed the significance of learning outcomes and the format for defining them. Defining learning outcomes is a crucial activity performed in the Design phase of the ADDIE model. Defining the outcomes helps the teachers and instructional designers to scope the content that is to be included as part of the instructional process, or in instructional materials. It also helps specify the domains (cognitive, psychomotor and/or affective) that need to be addressed through the instructional intervention.

Learning outcomes must be clear, focused, and measurable. To achieve this, you must ensure that they are written using measurable verbs. *Mager's format* is a framework used to write objectives in an effective manner, while *Bloom's Taxonomy of the Cognitive Domain* helps to peg the instructional material at an appropriate level.

In the next chapter, we will address the question – *how do we learn*? As part of this chapter, we will explore the three popular schools of learning --Behaviorist, Cognitive, and Constructivist. We will also look at how the principles of the three schools manifest in the learning process and in instructional materials.

Points to remember

- Learning outcomes are specified in the design phase of the ADDIE model.
- Learning outcomes specify what learners will be able to demonstrate upon the completion of learning. They are meant to communicate what exactly the learners need to remember/recall and what exactly the learners will do in real situations.
- For teachers, trainers, and instructional designers, the learning outcomes help to scope the content, identify appropriate learning strategies, and design relevant interactions and assessments.
- Mager's format is a popular framework that is used to write learning outcomes. As per this format, there are three parts to the learning outcome – performance, condition and criteria.
- Bloom's taxonomy is a classification that structures the thinking process from simple to complex. It helps us specify learning outcomes at the appropriate level.
- In K-12, higher education, and vocational training, the course or program goals are specified by an expert committee, and the instructional designers have to identify the learning outcomes at session and topic levels.

- In workplace learning, the instructional designers may work with SMEs to specify the program or course goals and define the learning outcomes at topic or module levels.

Multiple choice questions

1. Which of the following is NOT a component of the learning outcome as per Mager's format?

   a) Condition

   b) Cognition

   c) Performance

   d) Criteria

2. Which of the following is the ability to break down information into elements or relationships as per Bloom's taxonomy?

   a) Application

   b) Synthesis

   c) Evaluation

   d) Analysis

3. Which of the following is the ability to translate, interpret, or extrapolate information?

   a) Application

   b) Knowledge

   c) Comprehension

4. Select the learning outcome that violates Mager's format for writing learning outcomes.

   a) Understand the meaning of cognitive domain.

   b) List the various levels in Bloom's taxonomy.

   c) Illustrate Mager's format using examples and non-examples.

   d) Write learning outcomes using Mager's format.

5. Select the learning outcome that does NOT have a condition.

   a) Illustrate Mager's format using a graphic organizer.

   b) Write learning outcomes using Mager's format.

   c) Describe the six levels in Bloom's taxonomy.

Answers

1. b
2. d
3. c
4. a
5. c

Questions

1. Why is Bloom's taxonomy criticized? Explain with examples.
2. Describe Mager's format using examples and non-examples.
3. Distinguish between prescriptive and descriptive frameworks.
4. Select any topic and list the learning outcomes for the various levels of Bloom's taxonomy.

Key terms

- *Learning outcome*: The term used to indicate what a typical learner will have achieved at the end of a course, a session, or a class.
- *Knowledge*: Theoretical information acquired through learning.
- *Skill*: The ability to use one's knowledge effectively and readily in execution of a task.
- *Attitude*: This term is used to describe the feelings, emotions, beliefs, and values that an individual has towards another person or towards his/her work.
- *Performance*: This term is used to indicate what the learner will be able to do after a unit of instruction.
- *Condition*: It is a term used to describe the situation under which a learner's performance will be assessed.
- *Criteria*: This term is used to indicate the standards for measuring the learner's performance.
- *Bloom's Taxonomy*: It is a classification system used to define and distinguish between the different levels of human cognition.
- *Cognitive domain*: It is the capacity of an individual to think, or the intellectual skills.

- ***Psychomotor domain***: It is the capacity of an individual to apply physical skills.

- ***Affective domain***: It is the capacity of an individual to value, appreciate, and care.

- ***Descriptive frameworks***: These are frameworks that explain how things are, or how things work.

- ***Prescriptive frameworks***: These are frameworks that provide a template or a recommended procedure to complete a task.

- ***Knowledge***: It is the ability to recall specifics, techniques of dealing with specifics, and universals and abstractions.

- ***Comprehension***: It is the ability to translate, interpret, or extrapolate information.

- ***Application***: It is the ability to use abstractions in general situations.

- ***Analysis***: It is the ability to break down information into elements, relationships, or organizational principles.

- ***Evaluation***: It is the ability to judge something based on internal or external evidence.

- ***Synthesis***: It is the ability to produce unique communication, a unique plan/proposal, or an abstract set of relations.

Chapter 5
Designing Instructional Material

Einstein discovered the theory of *relativity*. The discovery may have seemed to happen in a moment, but in Einstein's own reckoning, it was the outcome of seven or more years of work. Most of us learned about this theory in school when our teachers explained it to us.

There are many of us who haven't attended any typing classes, but can use the computer keyboard fairly well. We can also safely assume that such people never consciously looked for or memorized where each letter is positioned in the keyboard, but their fingers seem to automatically go to the right letter when they type. How come? Of course, they may not have the same typing speed as those who have learned typing in a structured manner. And, light plays a role too; if you try the same in a dark room, it won't work.

Some of us recall a number of nursery rhymes, which we were taught in kindergarten despite not having recited a single one in the recent past. We may also recall mnemonics, such as BODMAS and VIBGYOR that we learned about when we were in middle school, though we may rarely make use of these consciously now.

Is it possible to understand something without someone teaching you, as in Einstein's case? And, how is it that we recall some stuff we learned as children but forget others? Is it because something was taught well and something was not taught well? Is it that simple?

Structure

In this chapter, we will discuss the following topics:

- Learning theories
- Andragogy and pedagogy
- Learning frameworks
- Motivation theories

Objectives

After studying this chapter, you will be able to describe how we learn, and differentiate between andragogy and pedagogy. In addition, you will be able to explain the frameworks that help us to develop lesson plans, session plans and online learning modules. Further, you will understand how motivation plays a major role in the learning process.

Introduction

Regardless of the delivery media being used or the audience being targeted, teaching or designing instruction should help the learners achieve their learning goals by making learning a simple and engaging process. What goes into making learning simple and engaging? How do you ensure this when addressing different audience profiles? Or, how can you make learning engaging and simple, regardless of the delivery media? An understanding of the popular learning theories (also known as schools of thought) will help us answer these questions, and make effective decisions when we design instructional sessions and materials.

Popular learning theories

To start with, let's once again focus on the variables and constants in instructional design, as shown in *Figure 5.1*. Before you design instructional material, it is important to analyze the *context*, which is made up of the following variables – the *audience* being targeted, the nature of the *content* being learned, and the *learning outcome*. It is equally important to understand how people learn, and what motivates them. Besides *memory*, a constant that was addressed in Chapter 3, *Designing the Outline*, these are the other two constants in the instructional design process – *learning* and *motivation*. Let's start with understanding the *learning* constant first.

Figure 5.1 displays the ADDIE model with the learning variables and constants:

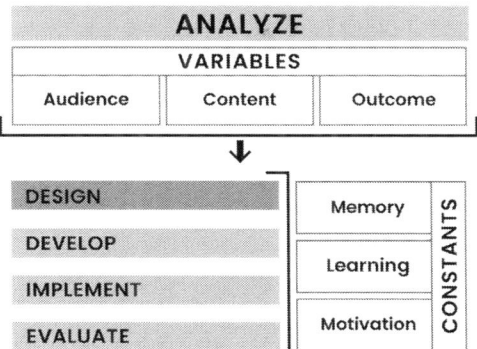

Figure 5.1: ADDIE Model (Adapted version)

Learning theories deal with *how people learn*. Understanding these theories will help you take informed decisions when you develop instructional material. As mentioned earlier, one of the problems in the learning field is an overdose of frameworks and models. And this is true of learning theories and learning frameworks as well. There are many frameworks that map to one or more of the learning theories. It is difficult to address every theory and framework, and many of these overlaps. Therefore, to keep it simple, we will look at the three main learning theories–behaviorist, cognitive, and constructivist.

Behaviorist theory

Remember the teacher who gave you smileys (☺) and stars when you answered a question correctly? Or, the one who made you recite important definitions and theorems over and over again, and chided you when you got it wrong? Well, they were both only doing their job! Though their approaches appear distinct, they actually adopted the same school of thought – the behaviorist school. According to the behaviorist theory, learning happens when a specific environmental *stimulus* elicits a correct *response*, and the response is *reinforced*.

Stimulus→ Response→ Reinforcement

The goal of instruction, as per this theory, is to *condition* learner behavior to *perform* specific *tasks* – hence the name, **behaviorist**. This school of thought proposes that knowledge and skills be presented sequentially and in a logical order. Thus, the behaviorist teaching-learning professional manipulates behavioral changes through reinforcement techniques, such as rewards and punishments. The learner's role is to passively receive information and practice new behavior until the behavior becomes automatic. Pavlov (1897), Watson (1913) and Bandura (1963) are known for popularizing this school of thought.

Cognitive theory

If you tell a three-year old that the world is round, she will, in all probability, perceive it as a flat cake, if cake is the *round* shape that she is familiar with. Even if you tell her that it is spherical, shaped like a ball, she will have difficulty accommodating that thought because in her scheme of imagination, it's not possible to stand on a ball without falling. That is the child's mental structure, and new learning will fit into this existing cognitive structure– new information will be *assimilated*. As she grows older and develops the ability to grasp abstract concepts, she will be able to understand that the Earth is indeed spherical – the cognitive structure will be modified to *accommodate* the information.

According to cognitive theorists, learning is an internal process. The human brain processes information, generates cognitive structures to be stored in memory, and translates it into behaviors such as understanding, speaking language, and solving problems. The information received by the brain through the senses, experiences a series of transformations until the data can be permanently stored in memory. Recall that we had addressed this in detail, in *Chapter 3, Designing the Outline.*

Sensory Memory→ *Short-Term Memory*→ *Long-Term Memory*

A person is pedaling their bike and suddenly hits the front brakes and their body continues to move, and they fly over the handle bars. You may recall this example, which your sixth-grade teacher shared with you to elucidate the principle of force and motion. You may also remember the technique to recall the number of days in each month taught to you when you were perhaps in the second grade –*every time you land on a knuckle, that month has thirty-one days; every time you land on a space, that month has only thirty days, except for February.* Instructors adopt techniques such as these to help their learners receive, assimilate, and accommodate new information.

The cognitive theory deals with the *internal mental processes* of the brain and how these processes could be used to endorse effective learning. Therefore, the instructor's role is to provide a mental model that the learner can follow. This theory propagates that concepts or tasks need to be first analyzed and then broken down into *learnable chunks*. Teachers are expected to organize and deliver information from the simplest to the most complex depending on the learner's prior schema or knowledge.

Constructivist theory

For most of us who are working for the first time, we find that we have to learn a lot of new things, which we were perhaps not taught either in school or in college. While some of these are learned through structured training sessions at the workplace, we pick up quite a few tasks and skills by working with others. Then, there are also those tasks which we simply *figure out* by ourselves. Learning new concepts and skills this way – by collaborating, actively participating, observing, reflecting and constructing knowledge – is labeled as the constructivist way of learning. In school and college, the many projects that we completed actively and collaboratively as a team are also examples of the constructivist way of learning.

Constructivist theorists are of the view that knowledge is constructed from experience and that learning is a personal interpretation of the world – *constructing* knowledge. They believe that learning is an active process in which meaning is developed on the basis of experience; and that, learning should be situated in realistic settings and testing should be integrated within the task, and not designed as a separate activity. Therefore, a constructivist learning environment encompasses *contextual learning*, *active learning*, and *collaborative learning*.

For constructivist theorists, the goal of instruction is to promote the construction of knowledge based on the learner's reality and prepare the learners to tackle varied situations in life. The instructor is considered as a *facilitator who probes, questions, and guides the students to think and solve problems through activities and discussions*. Learners are considered to be active participants in the learning process and control what they learn and how they learn.

> **Note:** The three schools of thought are not templates. They are descriptive theories that explain how we learn. Learning professionals are expected to know and understand these, so that they can design effective learning material.

Pedagogy

The term **pedagogy** refers to the way teachers deliver the curriculum content to a class. It is an academic discipline, which deals with how knowledge and skills are imparted in an educational context. It is the study of teaching methods, including the goals of education and the ways in which such goals may be achieved. The discipline of pedagogy is influenced by educational psychology and includes the scientific theories of learning, which we discussed in the previous section.

Andragogy

Andragogy is the theory of adult learning. Adults learn differently from children, and with increasing focus on workplace learning, there is a need to have trained professionals who understand how adults learn, and design the learning material to meet these needs. The term "andragogy" was first coined in 1833 by a German teacher named *Alexander Knapp* in an effort to categorize and describe Plato's theory of education. However, the term is most closely associated with Malcolm Knowles, an educator who had a massive impact on the adult-learning field. Let's look at some features of andragogy, as follows:

- One, as we evolve from childhood to adulthood, we become more mature and self-driven. While children need to be taught and guided, adults are capable of learning on their own. They prefer to be involved in the planning and evaluation of their instruction. This implies that independence and autonomy is characteristic of most adults and the learning experiences must be designed taking this into account.

- Two, adults also come with a wide body of experience. They gather this through their childhood and adolescence in schools and from the environment, and later from the workplace. This experience helps them to decode concepts, even if these are new to them. Therefore, as per andragogy, experience, including mistakes, should be the basis for learning activities in adult learning situations.

- Finally, adults are receptive to learning new things when they know that it is relevant to them. They don't learn something just because they have to. In other words, they look at how learning something new will help develop their skill set. They are motivated to learn only if they feel that it will help them perform their role better, either in the workplace or in life.

Table 5.1 summarizes the difference between andragogy (adult learning) and pedagogy (K-12 learning):

Parameter	Workplace learning	K-12 learning (children)
Cognition	Remains more or less the same	Varies by age/grade
Learning Outcomes	Skill development is the primary focus	Cognitive, social, emotional, and physical development are all given equal attention
Motivation	Intrinsic motivation matters more	Extrinsic motivation matters more
Context	Work context is given precedence	Socio-cultural context is important

Table 5.1: Differences between adult learning and school learning

Heutagogy

In *Chapter 1, Understanding Instructional Design*, we discussed how the learning ecosystem is undergoing a change, and becoming more and more demand based, and multi-modal and technology-driven. Given these changes, a new concept has emerged in the learning horizon – *heutagogy*. In **heutagogy**, the learner is given a lot of control in the learning process – from selecting the learning outcomes to identifying the learning resources and creating learning pathways. Since the learner makes key decisions regarding learning, it can be considered as self-determined or self-driven learning. The goal of heutagogy is independent and life-long learning, so that learners are adequately prepared to take on the dynamic demands of the modern workplaces of today and tomorrow.

Learning frameworks

A **framework** always helps us when we attempt something new. In the instructional design field too, we have numerous frameworks that guide us in the design of instructional material. In *Chapter 1, Understanding Instructional Design*, we looked at the ADDIE model, which is a framework for the **instructional design process**. **Learning frameworks**, on the other hand, provide a model for organizing the learning resources and learning events. These frameworks map to one or more of the learning theories that we discussed earlier. Let us look at some popular frameworks.

Figure 5.2 captures the relationship between the learning theories and learning frameworks:

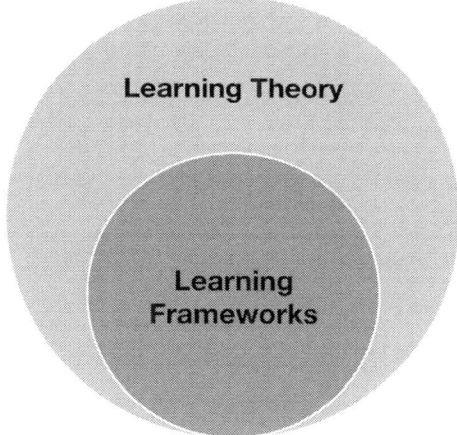

Figure 5.2: Relationship between learning theories and learning frameworks

Direct instruction

Direct instruction is the term given to describe learning material or learning events that are designed by the teacher, instructor, or expert by structuring the learning time and sequencing the learning content to address clearly defined learning outcomes in an efficient manner.

Barak Rosenshine, an emeritus professor of educational psychology, has identified some principles of direct instruction. In the first paper that he wrote, there were 17 principles, which were later filtered to six. These principles of instruction are picked from three research areas –cognitive science, classroom practices adopted by master teachers, and the cognitive support provided to students for learning complex tasks. The six principles are as follows:

- Review, checking previous day's work (and re-teaching, if required)
- Presenting new content/skills
- Initial student practice (and checking for understanding)
- Feedback and correctives (and re-teaching, if necessary)
- Student independent practice
- Weekly and monthly reviews

The preceding principles were designed for K-12 teaching, but may be applied to both vocational training and workplace learning as well.

Gagne's events of instruction

Gagne's events of instruction has its roots in the cognitive theory of learning and is very popular with all types of learning professionals. It is also not very different from direct instruction, as you will see now.

Robert Gagne, an educational psychologist, came up with this framework. According to Gagne, a learning unit (lesson, topic, chapter, or module) should include nine learning events. The nine events are based on the manner in which our brain processes information. It is important to note that Gagne's events of instruction is not a rigid tool, but a framework to guide teaching – so, it is fine to drop an event or two, re-order events, or combine a few, if required.

Table 5.2 describes the nine events:

Event	Description
Gain attention	Use any of the following to gain learner attention – story, question, video, artifact, exhibit, activity, demonstration
Inform learners of the objective	Share key learning outcomes
Stimulate recall of prior learning	Connect current topic with what was learned previously
Present the stimulus	Illustrate the topics that will be covered in the session (a diagram works well)

Provide learning guidance	Explain the information
	Provide examples & non-examples
	Demonstrate, if there is a procedure
Elicit performance	Pose questions
	Assign tasks/activities
Provide feedback	Confirm whether learner understanding is correct/incorrect
	If an activity is conducted, provide a debrief – Dos and Don'ts OR what worked and what didn't work
Assess performance	Ask questions
	Assign tasks under realistic work pressures and evaluate learner performance
Enhance retention and transfer	Provide opportunities to connect information with the real world

Table 5.2: Gagne's Events Instruction

Example 5.1 is a math lesson plan for K-12 mapped to Gagne's events of instruction:

Example 5.1	
Learner Profile: Grade 6	
Concept: Equations	
Topic: Introduction to Equations	
Gain attention	Show a big bunch of grapes with 10 grapes on one side and two bunches with five each on the other – with the question, "are the two sides equal'?
Specify objectives	• Define equation
	• Solve simple equations correctly
	• Given a situation, write it in the form of equation and solve it
Stimulate recall of prior learning	In a mathematical operation, the left-hand side equals the right-hand side. For instance:
	$5+2 = 7$
	$5 \times 2 = 10$
Present stimulus	An equation says that two things are the same, using mathematical symbols.
	An equal sign (=) is used
	Example: $10 + 0 = 5 + 5$

Provide learning guidance	Demonstrate how to solve an equation (use 2-3 examples)
	Problem: A number added to 2 equals 6. Find the number.
	Solution: Let the number be "X"
	X + 2 = 6 → X = 6 – 2 → X = 4
Elicit performance & provide feedback	Ask students to solve some equations
	Solve the following equations:
	1. X - 2 = 8
	2. X + 4 = 12
	3. X – 10 = 3
	After students complete the task, solve the equations on the board, and ask students to check their answers. Remedy incorrect understanding – explain what is wrong and why.
Enhance retention & transfer	Ask students to identify two or three situations from daily life and write equations for each of these situations. For example:
	You have to divide six chocolates equally among three friends. Represent this as equation.
	Let the number of chocolates to be given to each friend be X
	X * 3 = 6

Example 5.2 illustrates the outline for a module that caters to working adults, also structured around Gagne's events of instruction. Notice that in this example, some of the events, such as events 1 and 2, and 8 and 9 are combined.

Example 5.2	
Topic Name: Knowing your Customer	
Course name: Entrepreneurship Basics	
Target Audience: Working professionals	
Gain attention and stimulate recall of prior knowledge	Present a short scenario, such as the one below:
	"Think TastyBite, think cheese puffs! You love the cheesy treats. Even with your lips, hands, and keyboard smeared in TastyBite dust, you want more. Then why was the TastyBite-flavored lip balm a flop? With all the marketing and advertisements, the explosive sales did not come through! Where did things go wrong? You knew your target customers are women above 30. Was there still something you didn't know about them?"

Inform learners of the objective	• Define the term, customer • Identify the customer profile for your business • Create a demographic and psychographic sketch of the customer
Present the stimulus	Ask a question, such as the following: "Who is a customer? Why do you need an in-depth analysis of your customer?"
Provide learning guidance	Explain the key content points, such as: • Definition of a customer • The process of identifying a customer for a specific business • Significance of demographic and psychographic profiles • Difference between demographic and psychographic profiles • Techniques for creating the two profiles
Elicit performance & Provide feedback	Which of the following is the demographic information of a customer? Click the correct option(s). a) Income b) Hobby c) Age d) Spending habit Answer – a and c **Feedback:** Demographic information gives a statistical view of a population, which generally includes age, gender, income, schooling, occupation, and so on. Psychographic information describes the psychological attributes of the customers. These include values, interests, hobbies, lifestyles, attitudes, and so on.
Assess performance, and retention and transfer	Research and find out 3 products that failed to gain a foothold in the market because of not understanding the customer profile. Analyze the reasons for their failure and present it as a report.

Applying direct instruction and Gagne's events

Both direct instruction and Gagne's events of instruction work well in situations when very *specific knowledge* that is universally accepted needs to be imparted to novice learners, and also ensure a uniform understanding of this knowledge; for example, basic scientific principles that are universally accepted, or any content that is a derivative of these principles, such as *Universal Laws of Gravitation*, *Newton's Laws of Motion*, *Laws of Thermodynamics*, *Archimedes' Buoyancy*, *Machine Learning principles*, and so on. Basically, such content has an *intrinsic cognitive load* and is difficult to understand by novices, beginners, and intermediate learners. Hence, structuring and presenting the information first, followed by worked examples and finally practice questions make the learning process more effective and efficient. The frameworks are also applicable in any learning scenario – K-12, higher education, vocational training, and workplace learning.

Merrill's First principles

Merrill's First principles, put forth by David Merrill, a professor in an American university, is a popular framework used by instructional designers to design workplace learning. The framework is task-centered with real-world problems as part of the learning process. The idea is to show the learners the task that they will be able to do, or the problem they will be able to solve after completing a program or course. The framework also provides four instructional phases for presenting the new information to be learned. These are as follows:

- **Activation phase:** In this phase, learning professionals provide or encourage learners to recall a structure that can be used to organize the new knowledge.

- **Demonstration phase**: Learning professionals demonstrate what is to be learned in this phase. Depending upon the nature of content, the demonstration will include examples and non-examples, demonstrations, process diagrams with explanations, or behavior modeling.

- **Application phase:** In this phase, learners are given opportunities to use their new knowledge or skill to solve problems. The application phase is guided with feedback on what went right and what went wrong or could have been better.

- **Integration phase:** In the final phase, learners publicly demonstrate their new knowledge or skill through various activities. These activities may be in the form of reflection, discussion, debates, and/or application. In this phase, the learners are encouraged to explore new and personal ways to use this new knowledge or skill.

Applying Merrill's framework

Merrill's First principles is a learning framework that works in situations which have a clear overt task to be performed or a problem to be solved. In K-12, many concepts are taught to help students develop a solid knowledge base in a certain discipline. In such situations, it may not be possible to have an overt task or problem. For instance, when we teach students about the solar system in middle school, there is no overt task to be performed, or a problem to be solved. But, it serves as a foundation for developing higher-order thinking skills and the ability to process abstract concepts, such as gravity, in higher classes.

Example 5.3 depicts a session plan designed around the task of developing storyboards. Notice how the session is divided into four sections mapping to the four phases in Merrill's First principles:

Example 5.3:

    Topic name: Developing storyboards for online learning

    Course name: Introduction to online learning

    Target audience: Instructional design trainees in a company

Problem/Task: Develop storyboards

- **Activation**: Show sample book chapters and essays – highlight the structure in these and share that just like essays and book chapters have a structure, storyboards for online learning too ought to follow a structure.
- **Demonstration**: Share a storyboard template, explain the structure, and demonstrate how to populate the template.
- **Application**: Assign an activity that will require trainees to develop a storyboard – this can be done with the guidance from the facilitator.
- **Integration**: Ask learners to develop a storyboard in the workplace. Managers/reviewers can quiz the trainees on why a certain interaction is included, why a specific strategy is adopted to gain attention, and so on, forcing the trainee to reflect and respond.

Kolb's Experiential model

David Allen Kolb, an American educational theorist, came up with an experiential learning cycle, popularly known as **Kolb's model**. According to Kolb, adult learners learn through experience; therefore, it is necessary to design learning in an experiential format. This framework maps to the constructivist theory of learning. Also, it is basically a descriptive framework – which means that it explains *how most adult learners acquire new information and skills.*

> **Note: Please note that Kolb did not develop the framework as a template for scripting learning material; but we can use these principles as guidelines to do so.**

Kolb's model identifies four stages in the learning cycle. Kolb refers to these four stages as –*concrete experience, reflective observation, abstract conceptualization* and *active experimentation*. The phases follow each other in a cycle. The learning cycle, thus, provides feedback, which becomes the basis for new action, and evaluation of the consequences of that action. The following is a brief description of the four phases:

- **Concrete experience:** This part forms the *doing* component or, in other words, it involves experiencing the task.
- **Reflective observation:** This part flows from the previous one as it involves reflecting on the experience to analyze, and then discuss how the task was performed.
- **Abstract conceptualization:** In this part, concepts, principles, and generalizations are derived based on reflections from the experience of performing the task.
- **Active experimentation:** Finally, the generalized skills or behaviors are applied to new situations. In other words, the new skills or behaviors are tested out.

Basically, the overall idea in Kolb's model is to link theory and action by planning, acting out, reflecting, and relating it back to the theory.

Applying Kolb's model

Kolb's model has been found useful for workplace learning and in situations when the primary objective is to develop soft skills, such as leadership and team building, or skills that require judgment calls and decision-making, such as project management and change management. Also, the model works better for adult learners, who bring their own knowledge and experience into learning.

In *Example 5.4*, the topic of customer handling, to be addressed in classroom training, is designed around the four phases of Kolb's model:

Example 5.4:

       Topic name: Customer handling

       Course name: Consultative selling

       Target audience: Sales trainees in a company

- **Concrete experience**: Participants in pairs are asked to stage a role-play to handle an irate customer.

- **Reflective observation**: After all participants stage the role play, facilitator poses questions, such as what went right, and what went wrong.

- **Abstract conceptualization**: Participants derive conclusions such as customer handling guidelines and traits of a good salesperson with the help of cues and prompts from the facilitator.

- **Active experimentation**: Apply principles at the workplace.

> **Note: Kolb's model is a cyclical learning process, so a learner can start from any stage and not strictly from the concrete experience stage.**

As mentioned earlier, Kolb's model is not a template to be applied as is to a learning unit. It is a complex framework, one that is linked to four adult learning styles as well, and explains how adults think, and how adult learning styles may influence learning. Further, when we use this framework to design learning material, we must ascertain whether the content that is to be taught calls for reflection, interpretation, and generalization.

Comparing the frameworks

We looked at four different frameworks. These are all created by different education professionals, but there is a common subtext that runs across all four. If you reflect on each of these, you will find that there are three stages in all the frameworks. There is an activity or a set of activities that learners must engage in before we start teaching new information – let's call this as the **pre-teaching phase**. In the next stage, we will focus on teaching the new information by elaborating, explaining, exemplifying, demonstrating, and holding discussions – let's call this the **teaching phase**. Finally, we will check if the learner has understood the new concept by assigning some tests or tasks – let's call this the **post-teaching phase**. In short, one can identify three stages in the entire teaching-learning process, as shown in *Figure 5.3*:

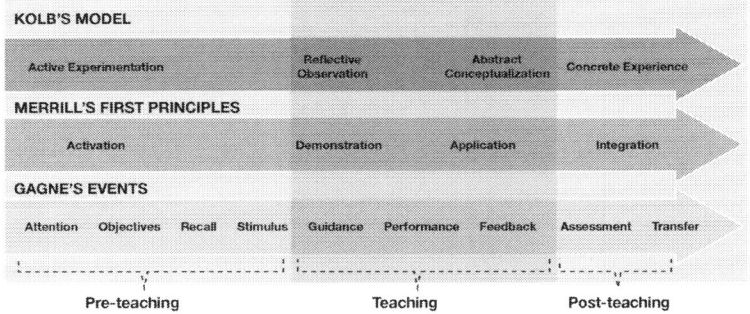

Figure 5.3: Learning frameworks – Comparison

Picking a learning framework

The question before us as learning design professionals is the framework to adopt in a given situation. To arrive at this decision, one must consider the variables involved – the *audience*, the *content*, and the *learning outcomes*. Let us understand this with the help of an analogy. Suppose you are planning a party, and you are out shopping for this. You have a certain budget that you plan to stick to for this event. The party is for your adolescent son, and he will be inviting his friends. The two *variables*, your budget and the party invitees, will determine what you purchase and how much of each item you will purchase for the party. Similarly, there is no playbook for designing learning material. You must consider the *context*, and all the *variables* involved before you pick a learning framework.

> **Note:** It isn't necessary that you always adopt a framework when you design instructional material. Frameworks help you to get started, but once you gain experience, you will find yourself designing the material intuitively with all the mandatory components – pre-teaching, teaching and post-teaching.

Motivation theories

Let's look at the next *constant* now –motivation.

Why do people learn? Or, why do some people grasp new information faster than others? Or, why is it that some of us perform better in certain disciplines? These are the questions that motivation theories attempt to answer. Before we learn about a motivation theory, let's get familiar with two terms that instructional designers, teachers, and trainers will frequently encounter. These terms are *intrinsic motivation* and *extrinsic motivation*.

Intrinsic and extrinsic motivation

Intrinsic motivation refers to the act of being motivated by internal factors to perform certain actions and behavior. This implies that there is no punishment or reward for the actions performed. Rather, the individual has a desire from within that pushes him or her to achieve a certain goal. On the other hand, if an individual performs an action or behavior because he or she will either receive a reward or get punished, then it is said to be **extrinsic motivation**. Intrinsic motivation is hard to achieve, and it develops over a period of time as a person's understanding of a subject increases, or as the person develops the competency to accomplish a task. As we saw earlier, when we discussed andragogy and pedagogy, adults are more intrinsically motivated than children.

Value-Expectancy theory

If you may recall, in *Chapter 4, Defining Learning Outcomes*, we discussed two types of frameworks – descriptive and prescriptive. The Value-Expectancy framework is a descriptive framework, since it addresses *what* motivates learners, and not how to motivate learners.

Norman. T. Feather, an American psychologist, who conceptualized this theory, describes motivation as the product of two factors, detailed as follows:

- **Valence:** The degree to which people value the rewards they expect from completing a task.

- **Expectance:** The degree to which they expect to perform the task successfully.

Simply put, the two factors can be reduced to the following questions:

- *Do I care for the outcome of this task?*
- *Do I think I can successfully perform this task?*

Also, the keyword in this theory is **product** – which means that if either one of the factors is missing, then motivation will be nil.

Figure 5.4 presents the theory in the form of an equation:

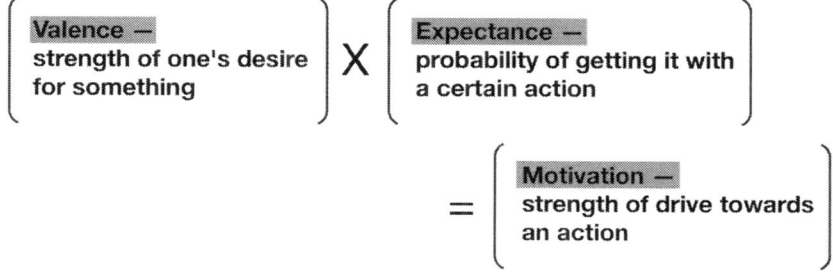

Figure 5.4: Value-Expectancy Theory of Motivation

Keller's ARCS model

The ARCS model was developed by John Keller, an American educational psychologist. This model, unlike the Value-Expectancy theory, is a prescriptive framework. It explains *how* to motivate your learners. The name **ARCS** is an acronym for **Attention, Relevance, Confidence, and Satisfaction**.

Table 5.3 provides a snapshot of the four components of the ARCS model, with a description of what each component means, and how to address it when designing instruction:

Component	What	How
A - Attention	Stimulate the senses	• Add surprise elements • Vary the elements of instruction
	Stimulate the brain	• Ask thought-provoking questions • Provide a problem to solve
R - Relevance	Make new information meaningful	Connect unfamiliar/new concepts with familiar concepts
	Make the material relevant to the learner's life	• Provide examples that learners are familiar with from their daily lives/workplace • Explain how the information will be used by the learner
C - Confidence	Present a degree of challenge through the learning material	• Provide a mix of problems and tasks ranging from simple to complex
	Allow students to estimate the probability of success	• Provide specific learning objectives • Present performance requirements and evaluation criteria upfront
S - Satisfaction	Provide opportunities to use newly acquired knowledge or skill	• Check Your Understanding (Quiz) • Practice Simulations • Hands-on Activities • Discussions • Group-work (in classroom training)
	Sustain the desired behavior	• Include feedback and reinforcements

Table 5.3: ARCS model

Do you notice the difference between the two frameworks? While the Value-Expectancy theory places the onus on the individual to be motivated, Keller's ARCS model provides learning professionals with techniques to motivate the learners. Clearly, the Value-Expectancy framework addresses *intrinsic* motivation while Keller's ARCS model addresses *extrinsic* motivation.

Learner engagement and interactivity

The discipline of learning, education, and instructional design has no shortage of terms and frameworks. Other terms for motivation are learner engagement and interactivity, which became popular with the evolution of online learning. While technology and media have contributed towards making learning accessible and engaging, it has also led to the emergence of a school of thought that believes extrinsic motivation as an essential ingredient in the design of courseware. And some of it is achieved by adding silly interactions and jazzy graphics that do not necessarily add any learning value to the content. Such strategies may not only be ineffective, in fact, they may even work adversely by increasing cognitive load.

Intrinsic motivation, unlike extrinsic motivation, is long-term specifically in adult learning situations. The more you comprehend a concept, the more intrinsically motivated you become. Stories, games, and jazzy graphics are no match for content that is designed with excellent examples, valuable insights, and elegant visuals, which communicate a concept in simple, but effective ways.

> **Tip: Just as a tapestry is created by weaving colored weft threads through plain warp, so is engaging instructional material designed – by weaving insights, examples, and visuals through the main content.**

Conclusion

In this chapter, we addressed the three popular theories of learning – behaviorist, cognitive, and constructivist. These theories help us make judgement calls, such as *should the expert sequence the learning process in a structured manner* or *should the learners construct knowledge with some support from the expert.* Further, we looked at four learning frameworks that map to one or more of these theories, namely, direct instruction, Gagne's events of instruction, Merrill's First principles, and Kolb's experiential model. These frameworks help novice learning professionals to present the learning material in a structured manner.

In the next chapter, we will look at instructional strategies, and learn how these are different from learning frameworks. The chapter will also address the commonly used instructional strategies to make learning material easy to comprehend and engaging.

Points to remember

- There are three popular learning theories, namely, behaviorist, cognitive, and constructivist. These theories describe how we learn.

- We learn something new when an expert teaches something in a structured manner. We may also learn something new on our own, by constructing knowledge from the environment around us.

- Our brain processes information in a certain sequence. Information is received by the sensory memory, processed in the working memory, and stored in the long-term memory.

- Direct instruction proposes that a piece of instruction be designed around six basic teaching-learning principles. This framework is helpful when you have to teach complex content to novice learners.

- Gagne's events of instruction is a popular learning framework that is based on the cognitive theory. In this framework, Gagne identifies nine events that can be included in a piece of instruction. This framework is also considered useful to address complex content to novice learners.

- Merrill's First principles is a framework which proposes that learning material should be designed around a problem or task, and the learning process should be structured around four phases. This framework is useful for designing workplace learning and vocational skills, where the goal of learning is to perform tasks in the workplace.

- Kolb's experiential model is a cyclical process which maintains that learners learn new information through experience. This framework is suited for designing courses that are meant for adults, and deal with soft skills or decision-making.

- Motivation plays a major role in the learning process. Motivation is of two types, intrinsic and extrinsic.

- Value-Expectancy theory describes motivation as the product of two factors, valence and expectance. If either one of these factors is missing, there will be no motivation.

- Keller's ARCS model provides a framework for building extrinsic motivation in the learning process and instructional materials.

Multiple choice questions

1. **Learning happens when a specific environmental stimulus elicits a correct response, and the response is reinforced. Which learning theory is this?**

    a) Cognitive

    b) Behaviorist

    c) Constructivist

2. **Which of these is NOT a feature of the constructivist theory of learning?**

    a) Active learning

    b) Collaborative learning

    c) Stimulus-Response learning

    d) Contextual learning

3. Activation, Demonstration, Application and Integration are part of which learning framework?

   a) Merrill's First principles
   b) Gagne's Events of Instruction
   c) Kolb's Experiential Model
   d) Keller's ARCS Model

4. As per Gagne's Events of Instruction, a lesson begins with _____.

   a) Presenting Stimulus
   b) Gaining Attention
   c) Providing Learning Guidance
   d) Specifying Learning Objectives

5. Which of the following is NOT a motivation theory?

   a) Kolb's Experiential Model
   b) Keller's ARCS model
   c) Feather's Value-Expectancy Theory

Answers

1. b
2. c
3. a
4. b
5. a

Questions

1. Describe the three theories of learning using examples for each.
2. A training program on leadership skills is to be designed for workplace learning. Which learning framework(s) will you recommend for this and why?
3. Do you think intrinsic motivation works better than extrinsic motivation? Why or why not? Support your point of view with convincing arguments.
4. A teacher wants to explain the concept of buoyancy to Grade 7 students. Which learning framework will you recommend for this and why?

5. Describe Feather's Value-Expectancy Theory.

6. What are the different ways to gain learner attention? Elucidate with examples.

Key terms

- *Behaviorist theory*: It is a learning theory according to which, learning happens when a specific environmental stimulus elicits a correct response, and the response is reinforced.

- *Cognitive theory*: It is a learning theory according to which learning happens when the brain processes information and generates cognitive structures to be stored in memory.

- *Constructivist theory*: It is a learning theory as per which learners construct meaning from their environment, and learning is active, contextual, and collaborative.

- *Pedagogy*: The term pedagogy refers to the way teachers deliver the curriculum content to a class.

- *Andragogy*: It is the term used to describe the adult theory of learning and is associated with Malcolm Knowles, an educator who had a massive impact on the adult-learning field.

- *Direct instruction*: It is the term given to describe learning material or learning events that are designed by the teacher, instructor, or expert by structuring learning time and sequencing learning content to address clearly defined learning outcomes in an efficient manner.

- *Intrinsic motivation*: This term refers to the act of being motivated by internal factors to perform certain actions and behavior.

- *Extrinsic motivation*: It is the term used to describe external factors, such as rewards, incentives, or punishment given to individuals to encourage them to perform an action, complete a task, or display certain behavior.

- *Valence*: It is the degree to which people value the rewards they expect from completing a task.

- *Expectance*: It is the degree to which people expect to perform a task successfully.

- *ARCS*: This is a model of motivation developed by John Keller. It stands for Attention, Relevance, Confidence, and Satisfaction.

CHAPTER 6
Developing Instructional Material

What are these?, asked the teacher, pointing to a chart. The chart displayed potatoes, carrots, radishes, okra, eggplant, and tomatoes. The entire class shouted in unison – vegetables. "*No*", said the teacher. Botanically, these are NOT vegetables. Suddenly, the entire class broke out in murmurs and whispers. The teacher, of course, had expected this. The students identified these items as vegetables because, in the smaller grades, it is what they were told.

This new information disturbed the existing mental schema of the students. They couldn't assimilate this because their schema was organized from a *culinary* perspective and not from a *botanical* one. Hence, tomato, eggplant, and okra were all vegetables; and so were potatoes, radishes and carrots. When the science teacher provided a botanical perspective, tomatoes, okra, and eggplant became fruits, while potatoes, radishes, and carrots became modified roots. Their schema was reorganized to accommodate this new knowledge.

What the teacher did in this situation is to specifically address a misconception that many students have on the topic of fruits and vegetables, as a result of what they learned in smaller grades. The teacher knew about this misconception because of the years of experience she has had in teaching the subject.

Addressing misconceptions is just one of the many techniques to help learners assimilate or accommodate new information. There are other techniques too, and the technique that we adopt will depend upon the *learning outcome*, the *target audience*, the nature of the *content*, or the *subject matter*. To identify the most effective technique, teachers, trainers, and instructional designers must answer some questions, such as the following:

- How should the topic or module content be treated or presented?
  - *This will depend on the learning outcome and the target audience.*
- What examples will aid the comprehension of the content?
  - *This will depend on the content or subject matter.*
- What activities will help in the understanding and retention of content?
  - *This will depend upon how you treat or present the content.*
- How should the content be visualized?
  - *This will depend upon how you treat/present the content.*
- What ancillary material should be created?
  - *This will depend upon how you treat/present the content.*

Structure

In this chapter, we will discuss the following topics:

- The various ways to treat or present content
- Ruth Clark's content-types
- Strategies for presenting content
- Significance of visuals in learning
- Significance of job-aids in workplace training

Objectives

After studying this chapter, you will be able to identify how to present content based on the five types of content recognized by Ruth Clark. In addition, you will be able to identify the most effective strategies for presenting the content. Also, you will be able to explain why visuals are a significant part of learning and the characteristics of good learning visuals. Finally, you will be able to describe job-aids and list the types of job-aids used for workplace training.

Introduction

In *Chapter 5, Designing Instructional Material*, we looked at how to *design* instructional material. In this chapter, we will address the next phase in the ADDIE model, which is *developing* instructional material.

Figure 6.1 depicts the ADDIE model that we have been referring to with the variables and constants that impact instructional design:

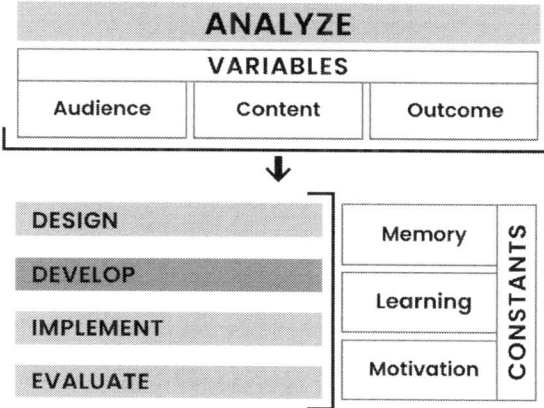

Figure 6.1: ADDIE Model (Adapted version)

Before we start, let's answer this question first.

How is the design phase different from the development phase?

Firstly, the *design* phase involves creating a blueprint that is guided by an understanding of learning theories and frameworks. The task in this phase is to finalize the sequence of instructional events (pre-teaching, teaching, and post-teaching). On the other hand, the *develop* phase involves giving form to the design or blueprint created in the design phase. This entails detailing each topic or module using certain strategies. The task in this phase is to flesh out the activities that fall under the *teaching* event.

Figure 6.2 shows the three learning frameworks we addressed in *Chapter 5, Designing Instructional Material*, mapped against the major events in an instructional sequence:

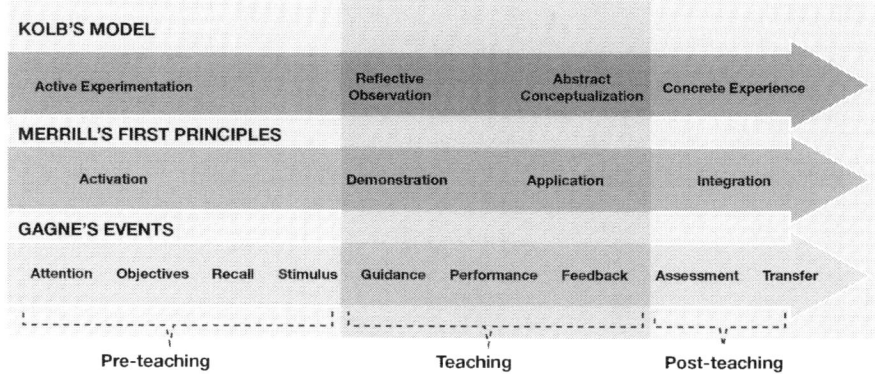

Figure 6.2: Learning frameworks – Comparison

Secondly, in the *design* phase, we are guided by an understanding of learning theories and learning frameworks, while in the *development* phase, it is important to understand content attributes or the nature of the skills to be acquired, and the effective ways to present content. This knowledge is known as **pedagogical content knowledge** (**PCK**), which teachers and trainers develop over time, and through experience. This knowledge helps them determine how to teach particular content in unique ways that lead to an enhanced learner understanding. Most often, instructional designers will not be experts in the subject matter or the task to be performed; hence they will not possess this knowledge, and will have to collaborate with the subject matter experts to better understand the content.

Table 6.1 summarizes the differences between the design and development phases of the ADDIE model:

Design Instructional Material	Develop Instructional Material
This phase involves creating the blueprint for developing instructional material.	This phase deals with detailing each topic, chapter, or module.
In this phase, the instructional sequence is defined.	In this phase, the teaching event in the instructional sequence is detailed.
This phase requires an understanding of learning theories and learning frameworks.	This phase requires an understanding of content attributes, or the nature of the skills to be acquired.

Table 6.1: Differences between the design and develop phases of the ADDIE model

Content-types framework

All things, living and non-living, tangible and intangible, possess certain attributes that help us categorize them. Recall the patterning strength of the brain that we addressed in *Chapter 3, Designing the Outline*. It is this strength that helps us assign attributes to things. For instance, mammals give birth to young ones, rocks are hard and brittle, and atoms are made up of protons, electrons, and neutrons.

Can the patterning strength of the brain help us categorize content? Well, the answer is yes. And, this has been done by Ruth Clark, a specialist in instructional design and technical training. She identifies five types of content, each with specific attributes in the book she has authored, *Developing Technical Training*. The content types are as follows:

- Fact
- Concept
- Procedure

- Process
- Principle

Depending upon what the learning outcome is, you can present content in any one of these ways.

Facts

There are 206 bones in the human body. Washington D.C. is the capital of the United States of America. There are seven colors in a rainbow. The solar system is made up of the sun and eight planets. These are examples of information that cannot be disputed, have been proved, and are known to be true at a given point in time. From a teaching-learning perspective, such information or content is meant to be remembered. When we present information like this, it takes the form of a *fact*. A lot of facts are covered in school and college education. In the workplace too, in order to perform certain tasks, employees may need to remember many facts.

An effective way to teach facts is by using a strategy known as mnemonics.

Do you recall, the acronym, VIBGYOR that your teacher may have shared with you in your schooldays to help you recall the order of colors in a rainbow? This is an example of a mnemonic. There are many types of mnemonic aids, but the most popular type is verbal cues that help us to recall facts.

Note: Mnemonics, other than verbal cues, are beyond the scope of this book; hence those are not explained.

The following example depicts the use of mnemonics in teaching and training:

Example 6.1: Mnemonics for facts

- **K-12**: **HOMES (Huron, Ontario, Michigan, Erie, and Superior)** is an easy way to recall the names of the great lakes on/near the Canada–United States border.

- **Higher education**: A popular mnemonic used to teach accounting principles is **DEAD**, which stands for **Debits increase Expenses, Assets, and Dividends**.

- **Vocational training**: In nursing, the treatment for a heart-attack is remembered using the acronym **MOAN**, which stands for **Morphine, Oxygen, Aspirin, and Nitrates**.

- **Corporate training**: **MIDGET** is a mnemonic that is used in the aviation sector. It indicates the checks to be performed after landing an airplane – **Master off; Ignition off; Doors/windows locked; Gust lock installed; ELT off, and Tiedown plane**.

Concepts

We often use terms to categorize things that display similar attributes. For example, food is a term that we use to categorize the things we eat. Book is the term that we use to classify all printed and bound reading material. Furniture is the term used to describe movable objects that we use to make a place suitable for living or working.

If we present information as an abstraction or mental formulation used to represent a group of things sharing common attributes, then we are treating it as a concept. In food, the common attribute is *eat*. *Printed and bound reading material* is the common attribute to identify books. In furniture, the common attribute is *movable objects found in homes and workplaces*.

Unlike facts, concepts need to be understood and not just recalled. Therefore, if we present information as a concept that is to be understood, we must define it, describe its attributes, and illustrate it using examples and non-examples.

The following example illustrates how concepts should be taught. Notice how each concept is defined and exemplified:

Example 6.2: Examples for concepts

- **K-12**: The ocean is a huge body of saltwater that covers about 71 percent of Earth's surface. Examples are the Pacific Ocean, the Atlantic Ocean, and the Indian ocean.

- **Higher education**: An asset is a resource with an economic value owned by a company, which holds the promise of a future benefit. Examples include cash, investments, inventory, supplies, land, buildings, equipment, and vehicles.

- **Vocational training**: Cleaning agents are substances used to remove dirt, including dust, stains, bad smells, and clutter on surfaces. Acetic acid, Borax, Ammonia solution, and Bleach are some common examples.

- **Corporate training**: Artificial intelligence is the simulation of human intelligence processes, such as visual perception, speech recognition, decision-making, and translation by computer systems. Manufacturing robots, self-driving cars, and smart assistants are some examples.

Examples can be used to make abstract concepts tangible, allowing learners to visualize the concept and deconstruct its attributes. When used to elaborate abstract concepts, examples help learners develop conceptual understanding of a topic, and provide a context or framework to connect new information. Examples direct the learner's attention to the features of the topic under study and help generalize the topic.

Non-examples

Non-examples too have a significant role in the learning process. While examples help to elucidate an unclear concept by providing an element of *similarity*, non-examples help to address learner misconceptions by providing an element of *contrast*. The patterning strength of our brain makes it easier to develop examples because our brains are wired to focus on similarities. But as we saw in the introductory scenario, the power of non-examples in addressing misconceptions is immense. Therefore, as teachers, trainers, and instructional designers, we must make an extra effort to include non-examples in the instructional material that we develop. Or, we may even task learners with identifying non-examples as it helps to stretch their thinking.

The following is a non-example shared by a teacher who is teaching classification of animals to students in Grade 5:

Example 6.3: Non-example in a lesson on mammals for school students

Animals that have hair, and where the females give birth to young ones are called mammals. For example, humans, cats, and dogs. But, platypus is a mammal, though it lays eggs. It is found in fresh water and estuaries in Australia. It is a small furry creature with a distinct bill and a wide tail. It is classified as a mammal because it has fur and feeds its young with milk.

In this example, the teacher is conducting a class on the classification of animals. She explains the characteristics of mammals and shares examples, such as dogs and cats. She also shares another example – a platypus. This helps students to understand that despite the presence of one distinct attribute (laying eggs), the platypus is still categorized as a mammal. She further elaborates that though the platypus lays eggs it is not an example of a bird or reptile. Thus, the teacher provides not only an instance of similarity (example), but also an instance of contrast (non-example). If the teacher shares only examples, then students will tend to memorize the examples. On the other hand, when she shares non-examples, students will try and grasp the underlying rules, and when they encounter a specimen, they will tend to apply the rules to classify it.

We can also integrate non-examples in activities, which involve creating a work output. For instance, sharing essays that do not apply basic principles of essay-writing as non-examples will help students avoid similar mistakes and understand what makes a good essay.

As stated earlier, most teachers will have pedagogical content knowledge. But not all instructional designers will possess it; hence identifying examples and non-examples may be a challenge for them. Therefore, it is important that when they interact with subject matter experts, they specifically ask them to supply examples and non-examples. Sometimes, the experts may not be academic experts and, therefore, will not know the significance of providing non-examples. In such a situation, the instructional designer must help the expert to understand what non-examples are and their significance in the teaching-learning process.

Procedures

Photocopy a document. Switch on the computer. Open MS Word. These are tasks that we accomplish by following a *clear sequence of steps*. When information is presented as a series of steps to accomplish a task, we are treating it as a *procedure*. **Procedures** are a common format for presenting information in vocational and corporate training.

Prepare a saturated solution of common salt in distilled water. Separate the components of a mixture containing sand, common salt, and camphor. These are experiments that students perform in schools – again a series of steps performed in a particular order.

Solve an equation. This is a procedure in mathematics, where mathematical operations are carried out in a sequence to solve a problem.

When we present information as a procedure, there should be tangible steps or tasks that learners are expected to follow. This may be done through demonstration, animation, or simulation.

Demonstration is a teaching strategy in which teachers and trainers show learners how to complete a task or solve a problem. This is a common strategy that is deployed in physical classrooms. When the objective is to depict how to complete a task, this strategy is usually accompanied by visual aids, such as models, specimens, graphs, charts, videos, etc. On the other hand, if the demonstration strategy is being used to show how to solve a problem, such as in mathematics, the teacher or the online module must walk the learners through each step in the procedure accompanied by a detailed explanation of each step.

> **Note: With the growth of online teaching and multimedia learning, now demonstrations are also designed in the form of animations. Animation is a method in which images are manipulated to create an illusion of movement in a sequence.**

Simulation is a teaching technique where learners complete tasks in an artificially created environment. This strategy is commonly applied when we have to teach learners to perform science experiments, use software, or operate an equipment. It is also a common strategy that is deployed for training in high-risk work environments, such as military, aviation, and medicine. In fact, aviation was among the first fields to deploy simulations, and flight simulators are commonly used for pilot training nowadays. Flight simulators resemble the cockpit of an aircraft, and use computer-generated images that mimic the pilot's view and the aircraft's motion.

The following example showcases how procedural content can be explained with the help of simulations:

Example 6.4: Simulations for procedures

- **K-12:** Getting students to build a galvanic/voltaic cell that generates electrical energy by selecting different metals and aqueous solutions through a simulation.

- **Higher education:** Using a simulation to familiarize core medical trainees with the bronchoscopy procedure which entails looking at a patient's lungs and air passages.

- **Vocational training:** Using mannequins to train nurses in performing routine procedures, such as catheterization, which involves inserting a tube as part of the urinary catheter insertion procedure.

- **Corporate training:** Simulating a video-editing tool in an online module to help graphic designers become proficient in the video-editing procedure.

Processes

Recruitment is the process through which employees are identified, interviewed, selected, and hired. This is a *workplace* process. A workplace process is a series of actions which are carried out across different departments in order to achieve a particular result. When you input data into a computer, the **Central Processing Unit (CPU)** decodes the action, and then delivers the output. This is an example of a *computer* (machine) process.

When we want to describe how something works, we present information as a process. Unlike procedure, a process is not an ordered sequence of steps. Also, unlike a procedure, when we describe a process, we must address the big picture – that is the system within which it occurs, such as a machine, body, environment, etc.

Processes need to be visualized, so they are best taught by using flowcharts, visuals accompanied with explanations (known as infographics), animations, and simulations.

The following example illustrates some strategies to present and explain processes:

Example 6.5: Animation, infographic, flowchart, and simulation for processes

- **K-12**: An animation that illustrates how clouds are formed and rainfall occurs.

- **Higher education**: An infographic to depict the series of actions involved in the content marketing process as part of a marketing course for an MBA program.

- **Vocational training**: An animation of the digestive system in a physiology course for training nurses.

- **Corporate training**: A flowchart depicting the employee recruitment process for new recruits in the Human Resources department of an organization.

Principles

Force is any action that tends to maintain or alter the motion of a body or distort it. Force is the *cause*; alteration of motion or distortion is the *effect*. The law of demand states that, if all other factors remain equal, higher the price of a good, lesser the people will demand that good. The price of the good is the *cause* and demand for the good is the *effect*. When we present information as a cause-and-effect construct, then we are treating it as a **principle**.

Such principles are best explained through animations that illustrate the cause and effect, or simulations in which learners can manipulate variables (cause) and see the corresponding effect.

When we present information to facilitate decision making, we include actions or decisions and explain consequences. In this case as well, we are treating content as a principle. Consider this –low cognitive load on the user interface results in a good user experience. Low cognitive load is the *design action* and good user experience is the *consequence*. Here is another example – opting to hold back a poor quality product that is scheduled to be delivered. In this case, a *decision* is being taken to hold back a product, which will have a *consequence* on the business.

Principles like these are best explained through decision-making scenarios and case studies, or stories. For online learning, the same may be designed as simulations.

The following example illustrates how simulations and scenarios may be used to teach principles:

Example 6.6: Simulations and scenarios for principles

- **K-12**: A simulation to teach Ohm's law shows how the equation form of Ohm's law relates to a simple circuit. Students can adjust the voltage and resistance, and see the current change according to Ohm's law.

- **Higher education**: Pulmonary patient simulators are used to simulate cardiac diseases – medical students can vary blood pressure, pulses, heart sounds, murmurs, and see the effect these changes have on the patient as part of the learning process.

- **Vocational training**: Models of the human body called manikins are used to simulate patients in distress. These manikins are controlled by someone behind a screen. For instance, a manikin may cough and his/her lips will turn blue, and trainee nurses have to make decisions and take quick actions.

- **Corporate training**: Simulations in which a series of situations is presented to finance professionals for decision-making with the objective to maximize share price, credit rating, and return on equity.

Let's now look at the features of scenarios, case studies, and stories, and see how these are different.

Scenarios

A **scenario** is a fictionalized account of a situation set in realistic settings. The context and environment are the real-world workplace, but the situation could be made up. Scenarios pose a dilemma to be resolved by the learner, a decision to be taken, or a problem to be solved. Typically, scenarios will include the following elements:

- A description of a problem and its context (real-world/workplace)
- A fictionalized account of a dilemma that is to be resolved, or a decision to be taken
- Supported by characters, dialogues, and conversations

Case studies

A **case study** is an in-depth study of one person, group, or event. Case studies are used to teach how information is to be applied in real-world situations, and the consequences one could face while doing so. They are popularly used in higher education, especially in business schools, law schools, and medical schools. In recent years, case studies have become a popular way to train corporate professionals too.

Case studies are often lengthy, addressing all the dimensions of the topic under study. It is high on facts, and is mostly supported with actual data and figures. Typically, case studies will include the following elements:

- A description of a problem and its context
- A dilemma that is to be resolved, or a decision to be taken
- Supporting information, such as data tables, exhibits, interviews, documentation, and so on

Stories

Stories are great way to learn, especially if you are addressing the affective domain. The high emotional content in stories ensures greater learning impact. The emotional content is what makes a story different from a case study or a scenario. Emotional content is added by way of a plot, theme, dialogues, or even characterization. Stories stay with people much longer than facts or statistics – the emotional content gives meaning and context to information. Typically, a story used for teaching or training will include the following elements:

- High emotional content
- Writing style is exaggerated for immersion and impact
- Presence of fictional elements is a must – plot/theme, characters, dialogues, and context

Table 6.2 summarizes the various strategies that we can deploy, depending upon how we present information to meet a learning outcome:

When we treat information as	Then use this strategy
Fact	Mnemonics
Concept	Examples
	Non-examples
Procedure	Demonstration
	Simulation
	Animation
Process	Demonstration
	Simulation
	Animation
Principle	Cause & Effect
	• Demonstration
	• Simulation
	• Animation
	Decision-making
	• Stories
	• Scenarios
	• Case studies

Table 6.2: Strategies to present different content types

Deciding how to present information

Knowledge of different content types and their attributes is very helpful even during the design phase, to identify teaching-learning strategies. This knowledge can serve as an effective input in creating the high-level design for a course or program.

Please note that the same information can be presented in different formats. How we present the information will be determined by the target audience and the learning outcomes for the module, chapter, or topic as identified in the design phase. For example, evaporation can be defined, and hence presented as a concept with examples. It can also be treated as a process and illustrated with visuals as part of a system, such as the water cycle. Finally, it can be treated as a principle too (heat is the cause and vaporization is the effect).

Typically, in lower grades within K-12, information is presented as facts, in the middle grades as concepts, and in the higher grades as principles. In vocational training and corporate training scenarios, information will most likely be treated as procedures, processes, and principles.

Visuals

Let's take a walk down the memory lane. Think of some information that you learned in your schooldays, and which you haven't used or revisited in a long time. There is a high probability that when you recall this information, it would have been accompanied by a visual because visual input is recalled more than verbal input. This phenomenon is very common and is referred to as the **pictorial superiority effect (PSE)**.

Visuals are extremely significant for teaching and training. Let us see why.

One, when we present complex ideas visually, the patterns within it become apparent and aid comprehension. Two, our brain processes both verbal and visual information. The two systems that process these are functionally independent – this means that there are two memory stores – a visual one and a verbal one. When we see content with accompanying visuals, two separate memory traces are created in our brains in the two systems. An interesting fact about this is that while the memory traces are separate, they are also linked. This increases the chances of recalling and retrieving this information. This process of combining text with visuals is known as **dual coding**. This theory was initially proposed by Paivio in 1971.

Visuals render value when they effectively complement the textual content. The following is what Daniel H. Robinson, a professor at the University of Texas, says about visuals:

"Visuals when used in a supportive way with text:

- Represent the text, providing additional nonverbal memory prompts;
- Organize and provide structure and form to text;

- Interpret otherwise complex text; and
- Transform text into pictorial images that can be stored more efficiently."

There are different ways in which we can integrate visuals or graphics in instructional material. Ruth Clark has identified a communication taxonomy for learning graphics. This taxonomy can help the learning professionals to identify appropriate visuals for learning content.

Table 6.3 depicts this taxonomy:

Visual Type	Description	Example
Decorative	Add aesthetic appeal or humor	• Art on the cover of a book • Visual of a general in a military lesson on ammunition
Representational	Depict an object in a realistic fashion	• A screen capture • A photograph of equipment
Mnemonic	Provide retrieval cues for factual information	• A picture of 10 forks stuck in a door to retrieve meaning of Spanish word for fork: Tenador
Organizational	Show qualitative relationships	• A two-dimensional course map
Relational	Show quantitative relationships	• A line graph among two or more variables • A pie chart
Transformational	Show changes in objects over a period of time	• An animation of a weather cycle time or space • A video showing how to operate equipment
Interpretive	Illustrate a theory or principle	• A schematic diagram of equipment • An animation of molecular movement

Table 6.3: Ruth Clark's Taxonomy for Learning Graphics
(Source: http://www.clarktraining.com/content/articles/MoreThanEyeCandy_part1.pdf)

Tip: A good learning visual is one that achieves the following – communicates the essence of the information presented through text; lightens text-heavy content by making information easy to comprehend; and retains the key message even when viewed without the accompanying text.

Storyboard

If you develop instructional material for online learning, then you will create a document known as *storyboard* as part of the development phase of the ADDIE model. Sometimes, it is also referred to as a *script*. This instructional material is an interim deliverable in the **development life cycle** (**DLC**) of an online course. The storyboard is written for multiple audiences – the *learner* who will take the course, the *subject matter expert* who will review the content for accuracy, and the *graphic designer/developer* who will design the screen layout and graphics to develop the final product.

Developing storyboards

A **storyboard** for online learning is written to be *seen* and *heard* by the learner, and call upon the learner to *perform certain actions*. Thus, we can identify three major components in a storyboard, as follows:

The **teach** component should address the primary content, which we just learned about in the preceding section – facts, concept, procedure, process, and principle. This is the key content for which the learner is taking the course. When you explain the primary content to the learner, when you cite examples and non-examples, when you demonstrate a procedure, and smoothly transit from one concept to another, you ensure instructional flow in self-paced online modules.

To **engage**, you will use scenarios, stories, case studies, or anecdotes that are relevant to the target learner profile. While these are not the key content per se, the presence of these engaging sentences is equally important for an online module to be interesting. Your story may also have dialogs or a mentor who walks the learner through the content. Or, you can have interactive content such as asking questions, and providing explanations in the form of feedback.

The **instruct** component addresses actual instructions to the learner to perform an action. For example, if you are teaching software features and functions, you ask the learner to click or select a tab or a button or a drop-down menu. You may also instruct the learner to type out an input to get an output. Higher-level instructions may include asking the learner to attempt an assessment or participate in a discussion via a discussion forum. The following example depicts samples of the instruct component:

Example 6.7: Examples of instruct component in a storyboard

- Select the Next button to move to the next topic
- Select the Play button to watch the video
- Select the correct option (for a multiple-choice question)

- Select a year in the timeline to learn how the Internet evolved

The three components, **teach**, **engage**, and **instruct** must merge seamlessly in a good storyboard to create what is known as instructional flow. While you, as an instructional writer, understand these as three different components, your writing should not be visible as such to the learner.

Storyboard format

The storyboard is mostly developed as a table in a Word document and includes the following columns:

- **Frame number:** Each row in this column represents a frame in the online course. If you are familiar with PowerPoint, you can think of a frame as a slide which contains all the information to be conveyed – including text, still graphics, and animation.

- **On-screen text (OST):** In this column, you specify the text that will appear on the screen in the online course. This is what will be read and heard by the learner. It is recommended that you present only a single idea in each frame/row. If there are sub-concepts connected to a single idea, include it as an interactive screen. An interactive screen includes a prompt for the learner to complete some action, such as click on some text/image, play a video, or respond to a question.

- **Audio narration:** This column is meant for audio text. You can write the content in this column using a conversational tone. In some projects, the audio script is exactly the same as the OST, while in some, the OST is a summarized version of the audio narration.

- **Visual and programming notes:** In this column, you provide instructions to the developer – the resource who will use an authoring tool to create the final online course. Therefore, you will need to provide visual notes, visual references, and programming notes here.

In addition, you will also give directions to the developer to synchronize OST with audio narration. This column must include details on what visuals to be shown, and notes for the programmer, such as whether it is a static screen or an interactive screen, what should be shown when the learner performs an interaction, and so on. This can be written informally, as directions to the online course developer/programmer.

Table 6.4 depicts a partial storyboard written for an online module on customer profiling. In this sample, the OST and audio narration are the same; hence, there is no separate audio column:

Frame #	Instructional Text	Visual & Programming Notes
1	Think Cheetos, think cheese puffs! You love the cheesy treats. Even with your lips, hands, and keyboard smeared in Cheeto dust, you want more. Then why was the Cheetos-flavored lip balm a flop? With all the marketing and advertisements, the explosive sales did not come through!	**Animation/image sequence:** 1. Show the cheetos packet with the cheese balls beside it for the first line. 2. For the second line, put a CRUNCH sound and make some cheese balls disappear. 3. For the third line, show a girl in front of a laptop with her lips, hands, and keyboard smeared in Cheeto dust. 4. For the fourth line, show the image of the lip balm and a 'Thumbs down' symbol on it.
2	Where did things go wrong? Maybe, they didn't understand the preferences of the customer when bringing out a new product. They forgot that what worked for the taste buds may not work for the lips!	**Animation/image sequence:** 1. Show the Cheetos lip balm with a question mark on it. 2. Fade in images of some girls and women (with refusing gestures) around it. 3. Retain the visual for the third line.

Table 6.4: Sample storyboard for an online course (without audio column)

Table 6.5 depicts the same storyboard written with a separate column for audio narration. Notice how in this sample, the OST is direct and the audio is in a conversational tone:

Frame #	On-Screen Text	Audio narration	Visual & Programming Notes
1	Cheetos as a cheesy snack was a big success in the market. Cheetos-flavored lip balm was rejected by customers.	Think Cheetos, think cheese puffs! You love the cheesy treats. Even with your lips, hands, and keyboard smeared in Cheeto dust, you want more. Then, why was the Cheetos-flavored lip balm a flop? With all the marketing and advertisements, the explosive sales did not come through!	**Animation/image sequence:** 1. Show the cheetos packet with the cheese balls beside it for the first line. 2. For the second line, put a CRUNCH sound and make some cheese balls disappear. 3. For the third line, show a girl in front of a laptop with her lips, hands and keyboard smeared in Cheeto dust. 4. For the fourth line, show the image of the lip balm and a 'Thumbs down' symbol on it.
2	What was the reason for the failure of the lip balm? Was it an inadequate understanding of the target customer?	Where did things go wrong? Maybe, they didn't understand the preferences of the customer when bringing out a new product. They forgot that what worked for the taste buds may not work for the lips!	**Animation/image sequence:** 1. Show the Cheetos lip balm with a question mark on it. 2. Fade in images of some girls and women (with refusing gestures) around it. 3. Retain the visual for the third line.

Table 6.5: Sample storyboard with audio narration for an online course

Job aids

Did you know? B-17, popularly known as the Flying Fortress was a U.S. heavy bomber used during World War II. However, the first B-17 flight crashed upon take-off. Investigations revealed that the Captain had left the elevator lock on, rendering the aircraft unresponsive to pitch control. What followed was a number of meetings and deliberations. These led to the conclusion that the B-17 pilots needed a checklist because the aircraft was too complex for a pilot's memory. And with the help of these checklists, the B-17s took flight again, and the rest is history. This anecdote conveys how a workplace problem was solved with the help of a checklist.

A checklist is an example of a *job-aid*. A job aid is an instructional tool that enables employees to recall or access the information they need to perform workplace tasks. Job-aids are very commonly used for vocational and workplace training and can be designed in any one of the following formats:

- **Checklists**: A document listing a set of tasks that needs to be completed as part of an activity/responsibility.
- **Infographic**: A visual representation of information or data, such as a step-by-step procedure with illustrations/graphics to complete a task.
- **Templates:** A sample of the real artifact with call-outs explaining the various fields and what should go into each field.
- **Flowcharts**: A process-flow diagram depicting input and output, and the various stage and entities involved in an organizational process.
- **FAQs**: A set of questions designed to address common queries and problems along with answers to these.
- **If-Then Tables**: A description of the problem or situation with the corresponding solution or decision.

Conclusion

In this chapter, we addressed how content must be presented at the topic, module, or chapter level when we develop instructional material. We learned that content can be treated as fact, concept, procedure, process, or principle. Depending upon how content is to be treated, we can present it using mnemonics, examples, simulations, animations, and scenarios, case studies, or stories. Further, we looked at the significant role that visuals play in learning and why visuals must be an integral part of instructional material. Finally, we learned about job-aids and their role in vocational and workplace training.

In the next chapter, we will learn about the Implementation phase of the ADDIE model. We will address popular terms related to online teaching and look at how instructional material should be deployed in online learning. The chapter will also address the factors to be considered when we conduct teaching and training sessions online.

Points to remember

- While the design phase involves creating the blueprint for developing instructional material, the development phase deals with detailing every topic, chapter, or module.

- In the development phase, it is important to know how the content must be taught. While teachers and trainers will know this, instructional designers must work closely with the subject matter experts to ascertain this.

- Ruth Clark identifies five types of content; each with specific attributes. These are Fact, Concept, Procedure, Process, and Principle.

- When we present information as points to be recalled, we are treating it as a fact. An effective way to present facts is by using a strategy known as mnemonics.

- If we present information as an abstraction or mental formulation used to represent a group of things sharing common attributes, then we are treating it as a concept. To present concepts, we must define it, describe its attributes, and illustrate it using examples and non-examples.

- Procedures refer to information presented as a clear sequence of steps. Procedures are best taught by presenting and explaining the sequence of steps that learners should follow. This may be done through demonstration, animation, and simulation.

- Processes are a description of how something works. Processes are best taught by using flowcharts, visuals accompanied with explanations (known as infographics), animations, and simulations.

- When we present information with a clear cause and a corresponding effect, it is categorized as a principle. When we present information as a principle, we should use animations that illustrate the cause and effect, or simulations. Information that involves decision-making is also presented as a principle and should be explained using scenarios, case studies, and stories.

- Visuals are extremely significant for teaching and training because when we see content with accompanying visuals, two separate but linked memory traces are created in our brains helping us to recall the information.

- Job-aids are very commonly used for vocational and workplace training and can be designed in a number of formats.

- Storyboards are developed as part of the development phase for online courses. Storyboards must include instructional text, and visual and programming notes.

Multiple choice questions

1. When you present information as facts, which strategy will you use?

    a) Example

    b) Simulation

    c) Mnemonic

    d) Animation

2. For which of the following information will simulation NOT work as a teaching strategy?

    a) Currencies of countries

    b) Digestion of food

    c) Evaporation of water

    d) Working of a printer

3. Which of the following will you treat as a procedure?

    a) Working of a CPU

    b) Formation of mountains

    c) Switching on a computer

    d) Condensation of clouds

4. Which of the following is a teaching technique where learners complete tasks in an artificially created environment?

    a) Animation

    b) Mnemonic

    c) Scenario

    d) Simulation

Answers

1. c
2. a
3. c
4. d

Questions

1. Differentiate between the design and development phases of the ADDIE model.
2. Describe the five different ways in which you can present information, giving examples for each.
3. Distinguish between procedure and process with the help of examples.
4. Why are visuals important in learning? Explain with examples.
5. Select content and context of your choice and develop a storyboard for self-paced online learning.

Key terms

- *Dual coding:* It is the process of combining text with visuals that helps to create two separate but linked memory traces in our brains.
- *Pedagogical content knowledge:* It is the knowledge that helps to teach particular content in unique ways that lead to enhanced learner understanding.
- *Mnemonics:* These are cues that help us recall factual information.
- *Simulation:* It is a teaching technique where learners complete tasks in an artificially created environment.
- *Animation:* It is a method in which images are manipulated to create an illusion of movement in a sequence.
- *Scenario:* It is a fictionalized account of a situation set in realistic settings.
- *Case Study:* It is an in-depth study of one person, group, or event related to a topic under study.
- *Infographic:* It is a visual representation of information or data.
- *Storyboard:* It is a document developed for self-paced online learning, which includes instructional text, and visual and programming notes.

CHAPTER 7
Delivery Strategies

Lakshmi's grandson recently gifted her a smartphone and also taught her how to use its basic features. Soon after, she joined a Vedic chanting class being conducted remotely by a revered teacher, referred to in India, as a *Guru*. Vedas are the oldest scriptures of Hinduism and comprise a number of hymns, poems, and prayers in the Sanskrit language. Vedic mantras are meant to be recited in a specific way with precise punctuation and intonation. The class was meant to teach this technique of chanting the mantras.

While the content itself is centuries old, the delivery method was contemporary – the classes were conducted virtually using the video-conferencing software. Therefore, along with learning the verses of the hymns and poems, and getting the pronunciation and intonation right, Lakshmi also had to stay alert to the Guru's instructions on using the software.

The Guru asked the remote learners to turn off their microphones at the start of the class. This was the easy part. However, when he asked them to switch it back on so that he could hear them recite, some of the learners struggled to follow the instruction. When the Guru repeated the instructions, it made learners like Lakshmi more nervous. She drew solace from the fact that there were quite a few who struggled the same way. Then, when she finally mastered this task, she found that quite often, she lost the network connection and missed her chance to recite when her name was called out. The Guru, on the other hand, had no way of knowing if she was still around or had dropped off from the virtual session.

Online learning has numerous benefits, but at the same time, it faces many challenges too. In this chapter, we will delve into the various delivery strategies in online learning.

Structure

In this chapter, we will discuss the following topics:

- Synchronous and asynchronous learning
- Technology used in online learning
- Online learning versus classroom teaching
- Virtual instructor-led teaching
- Challenges in online teaching

Objectives

After studying this chapter, you will be able to describe the following terms – synchronous learning, asynchronous learning, blended learning, and flipped learning. In addition, you will understand how software, such as **learning management systems** (**LMS**) and **learning experience platforms** (**LXP**) help us deliver online learning. You will also learn how the design and delivery of online learning is different from classroom teaching. Finally, you will know the challenges faced in virtual teaching and some best practices to address these.

Teaching-learning process

In *Chapter 6*, *Developing Instructional Material*, we looked at the *develop* phase of the ADDIE model. In this chapter, we will address the *implement* phase of the same model. This is the phase in which you teach a topic, conduct a session, or deliver training. The implement phase may be rendered in any one of these formats – offline, in the form of physical classroom instruction, completely online using the Internet, or a mix of the two delivery methods. Classroom teaching has been around for almost an eternity, so that won't be the focus in this chapter. Online teaching or **virtual instructor-led teaching** (**VILT**), as it is popularly known, is relatively new on the teaching-learning horizon, and that is what we will address.

Figure 7.1 depicts the ADDIE model that we have been referring to in all the chapters thus far. As mentioned earlier, we will now go through the *implement* phase:

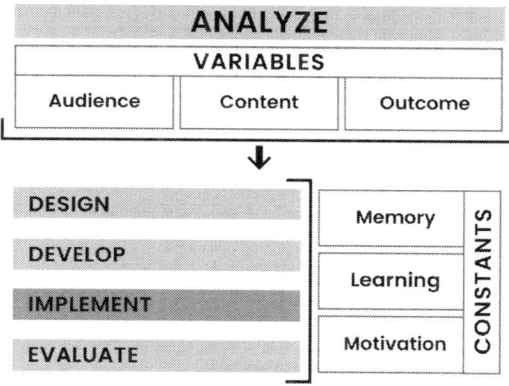

Figure 7.1: ADDIE Model (Adapted version)

Evolution of online learning

When online learning started as a mode of teaching, courses were delivered via **compact disc read-only memory** (**CD-ROM**). Soon after, with the coming of the Internet, similar courses were delivered over the Web, and this was called **Web-based training** (**WBT**). During this period, the course content was mostly related to **information technology** (**IT**) and was meant for training IT professionals. Educational institutions were yet to embrace online as a teaching medium during this phase. Since then, online learning has swung like a pendulum – from being made to seem like a magic bullet to being dismissed as the flavor of the month. Hopefully, it has achieved some sort of equilibrium now with trainers and educators becoming more aware of the advantages that it has to offer, along with its limitations. Online learning has now been deployed by many institutions involved in disseminating learning – be it K-12 schools, institutes offering higher education or vocational skills, and corporate organizations. We can, therefore, safely assume that online learning is here to stay.

However, this does not mean that online learning will replace face-to-face teaching in physical classrooms. While some situations benefit from online teaching, there are many others that require instructors to address students in a physical space. Consider the following situations – one where learners being trained to become medical professionals are expected to handle a scalpel with precision; or another where a person being trained as a mechanic needs to be guided by an expert to work with various engine parts. Last, but not the least, for school students, it is necessary to interact with each other in a physical space to help them develop social skills.

Whether it is to guide and mentor, or to clarify complex concepts, or teach something that will not be as effective in a virtual mode, the classroom model has its own strengths and will never be replaced.

While corporate institutions were the trailblazers in adopting the online medium, in the past decade, academic institutions too began to deliver a significant part of the learning process online. Online learning in these institutions took the form of homework activities for K-12, or videos of classroom lectures in higher education, which were shared online to help students revisit what was covered in the classroom.

But in recent times, when we witnessed the COVID pandemic, online teaching became the norm rather than the add-on. Hopefully, this event would have made those who dismissed online learning to be a fad, realize the value that it offers in terms of scalability and reach. On the other hand, those who thought that this would replace classroom teaching would have surely changed their stance after experiencing a host of problems ranging from poor network connectivity to distractions while teaching, and the absence of real-time feedback through body language and facial expressions of learners.

Types of online learning

A common misconception about online learning is that it takes the form of video lectures. However, this is only one form of online learning, where classroom lectures are recorded and then hosted through an Internet server, or the lecture happens in real-time using video-conferencing software. There is yet another mode of online learning, which requires careful planning and meticulous development of instructional material, which can be accessed by learners, anytime, anywhere. In this section, we will delve into these different modes of online learning, and the common terminologies associated with them.

Synchronous learning

Synchronous learning refers to an instructor or teacher addressing a group of learners virtually. Interaction between the teacher and learners and among the learners happens in real time. Typically, video conferencing software, such as Zoom, Microsoft Teams, or Google Meet is used for this purpose. The teacher may address the group in one or more of the following ways:

- Explain using a combination of video and *interactive whiteboard*
- Explain and present using presentation software
- Pose questions using third party interactivity tools or those available in the video conferencing software, such as *Poll* or *Chat*
- Conduct group activities using collaboration tools, such as *Breakout Rooms* available in the video conferencing software

Figure 7.2 depicts the various types of interaction in a physical classroom and the technology features that help us to replicate these in the virtual classroom:

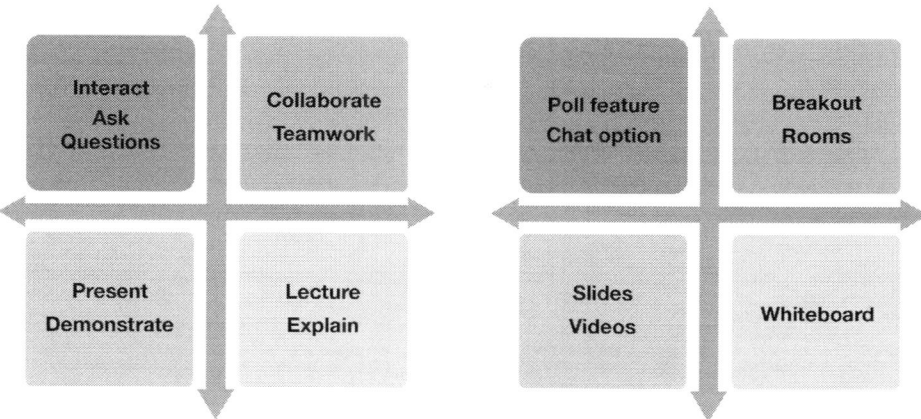

Figure 7.2: Mapping classroom learning with virtual learning

As you can see, online synchronous learning involves almost everything that students experience in the physical classroom. This is possible because most software providers have now included tools and features that will allow teachers to replicate the classroom experience. But, does VILT mean replicating the classroom experience? Well, we will get to that shortly – as soon as we have addressed the other modes of online delivery.

Asynchronous learning

In **asynchronous learning**, the teacher, the learner, and the other students are not engaged in the learning process at the same time. There is no real-time interaction with other people. This is also known as *self-paced learning*. Asynchronous learning is more flexible than synchronous learning as the learners can go through the learning material at their own pace and time. However, this type of learning assumes that the learner is adequately motivated. So, while it may work very well for adults and young learners looking to enhance their professional skills, it may not be a good stand-alone strategy for K-12.

The differences between synchronous and asynchronous learning is captured in *Table 7.1*:

Synchronous	Asynchronous
Teacher-led	Learner-driven
Group-paced	Self-paced
Same time	Different time
Instant messaging	E-mail or Discussion Forum

Table 7.1: Differences between synchronous and asynchronous learning modes

Flipped classroom

Asynchronous learning is adapted in K-12 by adding a little bit of structure to self-paced learning. This is popularly known as **flipped classroom**. As the term flipped implies, the typical classroom methodology of "**teach-homework-feedback**" is turned around to "**homework-discuss-feedback**". Direct instruction is presented through pre-recorded videos or presentations made available online, which students go through prior to coming to the class. The classroom time is used for delving and exploring the content in depth through activities and discussions. The idea behind the flipped classroom is to ensure that students actively participate in the learning process and in knowledge construction.

Blended learning

As online learning evolved, we realized that there are some situations that are best delivered using this medium. We also began to understand that for some learning outcomes, classroom teaching or training works better. Therefore, content came to be disseminated using both the modes. This mix of the two modes – online and classroom – is popularly referred to as *blended learning*. The features and essence of blended learning is captured well in the following definition:

"The term blended learning is used to describe a solution that combines several different delivery methods, such as collaboration software, Web-based courses, electronic performance support systems (EPSS), and knowledge management practices. Blended learning is also used to describe learning that mixes various event-based activities, including face-to-face classrooms, live e-learning, and self-paced learning."

Source: Blended-Learning-Models-2002-ASTD.pdf

Online learning technology

Online learning obviously isn't possible without technology. So, what is the software that is used to design and deliver instructional material? And how do these work? Let's look at that in the following sections.

Learning management systems

Learning management system (**LMS**) is the software that is used to deploy and track online learning. Typically, self-paced courses developed by applying the instructional design process are uploaded to the LMS, which are then accessed by learners virtually. So, LMS is a virtual library of sorts. Anyone with a login and password can access these online resources whenever and wherever. LMS acts as a repository with a catalogue of structured courses. It also makes administrative tasks, such as storing learner records and tracking course completion status easy.

Some LMSs have built-in eLearning *authoring tools*. These are tools that allow you to develop online instructional materials. For those who are not familiar with the term authoring tool, think of PowerPoint. Just like you can use the PowerPoint software to develop slides with text and graphics, authoring tools allow you to create learning material with text, graphics, interactions, audio, video, and animation. Some authoring tools also come with a library of images.

> **Note: LMSs can be proprietary or open source. Open source means that you can use the software without purchasing a license. Moodle is an example of an open-source LMS.**

Learning experience platforms

The increasing role of social media in our day-to-day lives has impacted the way we learn as well. What started off as virtual spaces to connect, morphed into virtual spaces to learn and share. *LinkedIn*, *Pinterest*, and *Twitter* became platforms where members could learn, share, and publish content. YouTube began to be increasingly used by people to publish the videos they created – especially "*How To*" tutorials. Added to this, smart phones made it easy to access and share content anytime, anywhere. So, basically, content authoring and publishing that happened within a closed system like the LMS were thrown open to anyone who wished to create and share content.

LMSs didn't provide the collaboration and learning features that social networking platforms offered. Neither did it track data related to these informal means of learning. Last, but not the least, most LMSs were not compatible with mobile phones. It is in this scenario, that **Learning experience platforms** (**LXP**) emerged. Unlike LMS, which is a closed platform, where administrators control content, LXPs allow users to aggregate and curate content. It offers greater user control than the traditional LMS. In addition, it can be integrated with other systems, such as human resource systems, and is also mobile compatible. Also, unlike LMS, LXPs are designed to track informal and social learning as well. In this type of learning, students or learners learn from each other, as against learning from a teacher or a formal course. In other words, individuals collectively seek and find relevant content from various sources. Some LXPs are also **Artificial Intelligence** (**AI**) driven.

> **Note: LXPs allow users, including the learners to find existing content that is related to a topic or subject and add it to an existing curriculum. This strategy is known as content curation. An example of curation that we encounter in everyday life is the use of hash tags in social media sites.**

Figure 7.3 captures the difference between the two systems:

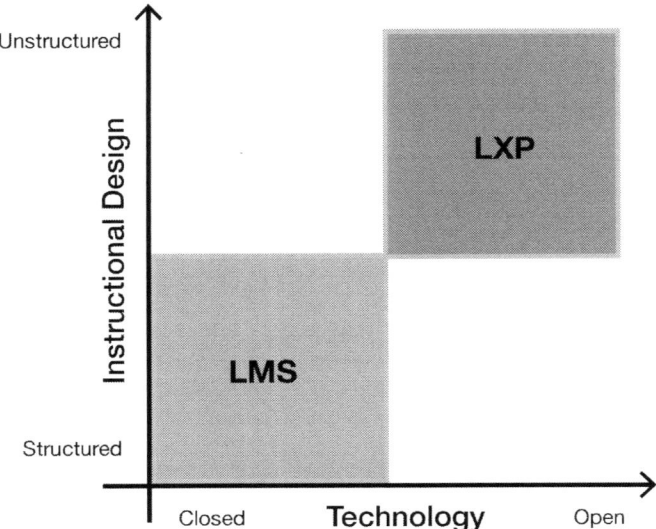

Figure 7.3: *LMS and LXP – A Comparison*

Comparing asynchronous online learning and classroom teaching

If you are an instructional designer, you would have perhaps designed material for both classroom-training and asynchronous online learning. But, if you have been a trainer or a teacher, you may have only designed lesson and session plans using which you conducted classes.

Let's take a detailed look at how the design of online learning materials differs from routine classroom teaching. Understanding the differences is important and will help you deploy the right processes and teams to design material that optimizes the strength of the medium.

Note: Classroom training in corporate organizations is popularly known as Instructor-led Training (ILT).

Table 7.2 provides a comparison of the two modes:

Parameter	Online self-paced learning	Classroom Teaching
Development process	Development process may be longer since the implementation phase (ADDIE) requires media and technology support.	Development process is shorter since the implementation phase requires less media support and almost no technology support.
Instructional Materials	• Storyboards/Scripts with visual and programming notes	• PowerPoint Slides • Instructor Guide • Participant Guide • Lesson/Session Plan
Resources involved in developing	• Instructional Designers • Subject Matter Experts • Editors • Graphic Artists • Technology professionals	• Instructional Designers • Trainers/Teachers
Instructional clarity	• Explanations must be self-contained • The content must be clear, concise, and written in simple language. • Illustrations should be adequately explained using voice over or text.	If some content is unclear, the facilitator has an opportunity to clarify then and there.
Interactions	Interactions occur in real time only with the content. Interactions with other learners and/or facilitator are through the online platform.	Interactions occur in real time with: • content • other learners • facilitator
Reference Material	Online courses are not easy for referencing. Hence, it is important to provide downloadable material that can be easily referenced.	Guides are available to the learner to keep and can be used as reference material later.
Assessments	Objective assessments are easy to administer and score.	Subjective assessments and assignments can be administered.

Table 7.2: Comparing online learning with classroom teaching

> **Tip: If you are a subject matter expert and you also know how to use an authoring tool, you can create self-paced online material on your own without depending upon graphic designers and developers.**

Virtual instructor-led teaching

Now that we have covered the different online delivery modes, let us look at how to exploit the online medium optimally.

The key factor to keep in mind with regard to **virtual instructor-led training** (VILT) is that it isn't about replicating classroom teaching. Teaching and learning virtually places a higher cognitive load on the teacher and student as both have to handle software and other technology issues along with teaching/learning. If you have attended or conducted a virtual teaching session, you will understand this better.

Working of VILT

Just think of the last time you attended a virtual training session. If the session was just a monologue by the teacher – that is speaking via video – then the only challenge you would have faced was to sit through the session without getting distracted, provided that the teacher or trainer was a great orator, and had something interesting to say for the entire duration.

However, if the teacher had designed an interactive session, then you would have had to complete some tasks, such as read an article from a Web page, respond to an objective question, or answer a quiz question verbally when called upon to do so. In the first case, you may have struggled to copy and paste the link she shared with you through the chat window. In the second case, you may have spent a few seconds trying to locate the microphone icon on your screen and switching it on before you answered the question. And, in all probability you would have also spoken into the microphone a couple of times before you realized that you hadn't switched it on. During this time, the teacher may have wondered whether you had dropped off from the session and, thus, passed on the question to another student.

Now, suppose you are the facilitator – the one conducting the session. In this case, you have to teach the content, and remember to use the relevant controls in the software at the appropriate time. Even if you create the material in advance using presentation software, what happens in real time cannot be predicted. What's more; you can't see your learners if they have switched off the video to save bandwidth. Hence, you can't modify your talking points on the fly, as and when you witness the blank looks on the face of your learners, which is how you do it in the physical classroom.

Collaborating in VILT sessions

While simple online interactions significantly increase cognitive load, online collaborations increase it even more. Nowadays, most video conferencing software come with a feature that allows you to assign group work to participants. This feature is known as *Breakout Rooms*. Perhaps, it gets this moniker because facilitators can break a class into groups and assign them virtual rooms to collaborate. When facilitators want to assign group work to participants, they can split them into separate sessions, either manually or automatically. This can be pre-planned or done in real time. The following is a list of things that you can do with *Breakout Rooms*:

- Open these when you want to get started with an activity.
- Close these when you want to close an activity.
- Give names to each room, such as Group A, Group B and so on.
- Send messages and prompts to groups during an activity, such as a time warning.
- Pop in and out of these rooms to supervise, or broadcast a message.
- Schedule group activities to open and close automatically.

Using breakout rooms

Using breakout rooms is not without any challenges. At times, breakout groups spend several precious minutes from the allocated duration to discuss instructions for completing the task. This eats into the total allocated time for the task, not allowing the groups to complete the task. In addition, as the teacher-organizer, when you pop in and out of these rooms, the participants may get distracted. If you send a message to all groups, the pop-up on the screen can add to the cognitive load. Further, the opaqueness of the virtual medium in reading student expressions and body language make it difficult for the teacher-organizer to quickly clarify doubts that some participants may have. These challenges may be addressed in the following ways:

- Before starting the collaborative activity, explain the procedure to complete it by sharing the file which includes instructions for completing the activity. You can use the Share feature of the video conferencing tool to do this. Send this file to group leaders after you complete the explanation.

- You may also walk the learners through the instructions in the document. This will help them raise queries to clarify doubts.

- You may either email the file to group leaders, prior to your session, or post the URL to the file after you complete explaining the activity. Group leaders can be tasked with filling in the responses, which they can share through their screen.

Planning for online teaching

Consider an example. Suppose an institution offers a certification program in instructional design and delivers it as blended learning. Learners have to go through some self-paced online modules hosted on the LMS, attend a few VILT sessions, which are conducted by the subject matter expert, and then submit an assignment. This is a month-long program with a standard format and a mix of instructional events for each day.

Figure 7.4 depicts the instructional flow for one day:

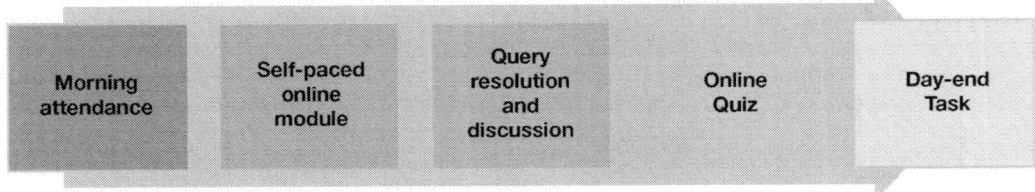

Figure 7.4: Blended learning – Session Flow

As we can observe, this program includes both synchronous and asynchronous activities. *Table 7.3* provides a detailed description of each instructional event:

Event	Mode	Duration	How?
Morning Attendance	Synchronous	30 minutes	Facilitator assigns learning tasks for the day, and recaps concepts addressed the previous day
Self-paced Learning	Asynchronous	1 hour	Learners go through the self-paced learning material. This can be a mix of the following: • Videos • Animations • Infographics • Articles • Interactive exercises
Explanation & Interaction with Trainer	Synchronous	1 hour	Elaborates concepts that require further explanation, clarifies doubts, and explains the assignment for the day

Event	Mode	Duration	How?
Hands-on Activity	Asynchronous	2 hours	The activities will range from simple individual exercise to some group work. Learners can be given a **digital handbook,** which contains all the instructions and material for the activities.
Assignment Submission & Day-end Online Quiz	Asynchronous	30 minutes	Learners will submit their assignments and take a short online quiz on the topics covered in the day.

Table 7.3: Session plan for blended learning

You can see how a day-long session in the virtual mode can be addressed through a mix of synchronous and asynchronous activities. Therefore, when you plan to conduct a virtual session, the following are a few things that you can do to make sure that learning is effective and collaborative activities are seamless:

- Address some part through the asynchronous mode as self-paced learning or flipped classroom.

- Plan some offline activities in case of disruptions due to technical issues.

- Give breaks to being online; provide some tasks that can be completed offline before meeting online again.

- Share clearly documented guidelines beforehand for interactions and collaborations.

Conclusion

In this chapter, we looked at the *Implement* phase of the ADDIE model, which deals with the various modes in which learning can be delivered. We addressed virtual classrooms facilitated by teachers or trainers, known as synchronous learning. We also learned about asynchronous or self-paced learning, blended learning, and flipped classrooms. In addition, we compared online teaching with classroom learning, and addressed the challenges faced in virtual teaching. Finally, we covered some best practices that may be deployed in virtual teaching.

In the next chapter, we will go through the last phase of the ADDIE model, which is *Evaluate*. We will address the various types of assessment strategies that can be used to evaluate learners and the learning process.

Points to remember

- In the *Implement* phase of the ADDIE model, you teach using the materials that were designed and developed in the earlier phases.

- Teaching can be either offline, in physical classrooms, or online via the Internet using software that helps you deploy content and/or collaborate virtually.

- Online teaching can be done in different ways. Learners may attend a session being conducted by a facilitator in real time virtually (synchronous learning), or go through self-paced courses (asynchronous learning).

- Self-paced online courses must be carefully designed by a team comprising of instructional designers, subject matter experts, graphic designers, and technology professionals.

- Software has made it possible to include, in the online mode, most learning events that are deployed in a physical classroom.

- Virtual instructor-led teaching must not be a replication of the classroom mode. Online learning must be carefully planned to optimize the strengths of the medium. A mix of synchronous and asynchronous learning is the best way to facilitate online learning.

Multiple choice questions

1. A facilitator uses video-conferencing software to conduct a virtual class. Learners can interact with each other, and with the facilitator in real time. What is this type of online learning called?

    a) Synchronous learning

    b) Self-paced learning

    c) Blended learning

    d) Flipped learning

2. A teacher asks her class to go through a video on photosynthesis from home. The next day, she conducts a discussion on the topic in class. What is the term used for this strategy?

a) Synchronous learning

b) Flipped learning

c) Social learning

3. **For a virtual training session, a facilitator wants to assign the participants a group activity. Which software feature will allow her to create groups?**

   a) Whiteboard

   b) Instant Messaging

   c) Breakout Rooms

4. **How does virtual teaching/online learning impact cognitive load?**

   a) It increases cognitive load

   b) It decreases cognitive load

   c) Cognitive load remains the same

Answers

1. a
2. b
3. c
4. a

Questions

1. Describe the implement phase of the ADDIE model.

2. Explain the term asynchronous learning with the help of examples.

3. How is classroom teaching different from virtual teaching? List all the differences.

4. Write a short paragraph describing the challenges of teaching in the virtual mode and how these challenges can be addressed.

Key terms

- *Synchronous learning:* This refers to an instructor or teacher addressing a group of learners virtually, with interactions occurring in real time.

- *Whiteboard:* It is an area common to several users or applications, where they can exchange information, in particular as handwriting or graphics.

- *Breakout room:* It is a small meeting room or a separate part of a virtual training where a small group can complete an assignment or discuss a specific topic before returning to the main training.

- *Asynchronous learning:* In this type of learning, the teacher, the learner, and the other learners are not engaged in the learning process at the same time, and there is no real-time interaction with other people. This is also known as self-paced learning.

- *Flipped classroom:* A strategy where the typical classroom methodology of "teach-homework-feedback" is turned around to "homework-discuss-feedback".

- *Blended learning:* This term is used to describe a solution that combines several different delivery methods, such as online and offline, and various learning events, such as lectures, assessments, assignments etc.

- *Social Learning:* This term is defined as learning from each other, as against learning from a formal course. Collectively, individuals can seek and find relevant content from various sources.

- *Learning Management Systems:* This is the software that is used by administrators and facilitators to deploy and track formal online learning.

- *Learning Experience Platforms:* This is the software that allows learners and facilitators to aggregate and curate content, and track both formal and informal learning.

- *Curate:* A process that involves finding, grouping, organizing, and sharing the best and most relevant content on a specific topic. Curation may be automated or manual.

- *Authoring tool:* This is a type of software that helps you create learning material with text, graphics, interactions, audio, video, and animation.

CHAPTER 8
Assessment Strategies

During Satya's annual performance appraisal, his supervisor identified time management as an area of improvement. Subsequently, he was asked to go through an online self-paced module on the subject. Despite doing so, he didn't improve even a fraction of his skills in the area. Being a person who takes every responsibility rather seriously, he wondered why his skills remained the same. After all, he did score 98% in the online assessment.

So, he sat down and listed all the question items from the online assessment – the need for managing time, activity enhancers and time wasters, and best practices in time management. By putting it all down on paper, the problem revealed itself to him. All that the module covered and assessed him on was *declarative knowledge*, which is *what he knows* about time management. The more appropriate part – *how to manage time*, which is *procedural knowledge*, was presented as best practices and tested through a few multiple-choice questions. There was nothing to assess him on this part. Basically, the assessment itself wasn't *valid*.

Designing assessments is an integral part of the instructional design process. Assessments, at various levels, test the learner's ability to retrieve, reflect, assimilate, and apply the acquired knowledge or skills. Designing effective assessments is both art and science.

The primary purpose of assessment is to improve the students' learning and teachers' teaching. A good assessment helps teachers and trainers gather evidence of how much learning has happened, and that helps them make future instructional decisions and close gaps. In addition, assessments also serve as a roadmap for learners. *"How much have I learnt and how further do I need to go?"* Therefore, the questions used to assess should ensure that these tacit objectives that teachers, trainers, and learners have, are also met. This chapter will cover the purpose of assessments and the different types of assessments that can be administered as part of the learning process, and check whether the instructional material and its delivery have been effective.

Structure

In this chapter, we will discuss the following topics:

- Purpose of assessments
- Formative and summative assessments
- Question types for assessing declarative knowledge
- Tools for assessing procedural knowledge
- Kirkpatrick's model

Objectives

After studying this chapter, you will be able to describe the purpose of assessment, and distinguish between formative and summative assessments. In addition, you will learn how to identify the different types of questions that can be used to assess declarative knowledge. Further, you will understand the different types of assessment tools that can be used to check procedural knowledge. Finally, you will learn about Kirkpatrick's model of evaluation.

Understanding evaluation

Evaluation is the process of making judgments based on certain criteria and evidence. This is the final phase in the ADDIE model. As per the ADDIE model, evaluation implies two things – one, evaluation of the learner, and two, evaluation of the instructional material or the teaching/training process.

As you can see in *Figure 8.1*, evaluation is the final phase in the ADDIE model:

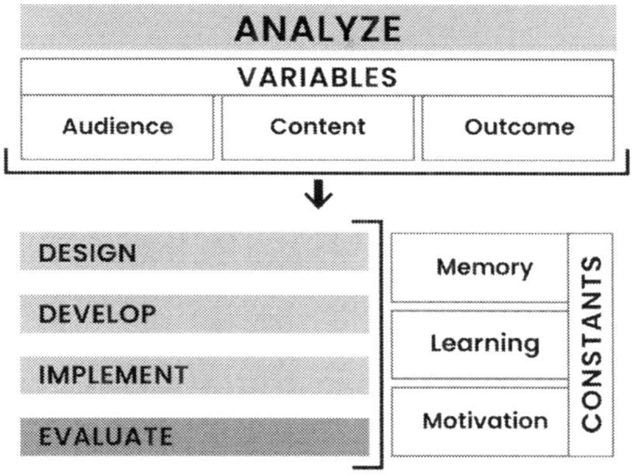

Figure 8.1: ADDIE model (Adapted version)

As a learning practitioner, you may have heard many terms associated with evaluation, such as assessment, test, quiz, knowledge-check, check your understanding, and more. What do these mean? Are they synonymous? Or do they represent different things? Let's address that first.

Types of assessments

A **test** is used to examine someone's knowledge of something to determine what he or she knows or has learned. Testing measures the level of skill or knowledge that has been reached. A **quiz** is usually a short test, and often doesn't have a huge impact on the learner's grades as compared to a test. The terms, **Check Your Understanding** or **Knowledge Check** are commonly used in online courses. They are similar to a quiz that is used in educational settings.

Evaluation, as referred to in the ADDIE model, is yet another term that is commonly used, and is different from assessment. The purpose of evaluation is to judge. However, the purpose of assessment is not to judge, but to help learners improve their performance. In other words, **assessment** is the process of finding out whether the learners are making progress with learning or not, and is only a subset of evaluation. It involves collecting, reviewing, and using data, for improving current performance. Some educationists refer to the two as **formative assessment** (assessment), and **summative assessment** (evaluation). In the following section, we will address these in detail.

Formative and summative assessments

Formative assessment is supposed to help learners retrieve information from memory so as to strengthen learning. It is assessment *for* learning. The practice of retrieving new concepts from memory enables learning and ensures durable retention.

Summative assessment (evaluation) is the assessment *of* learning and is presented as a periodic report. It is designed to provide information not only to teachers and learners, but also to those who are not directly involved in daily learning and teaching, such as the **human resources** (**HR**) division in corporate organizations, and the parents and school boards in educational institutions.

Table 8.1 depicts a comparison of formative and summative assessments:

Parameter	Formative assessment	Summative assessment/evaluation
What?	Formative assessment is the assessment *for* Learning.	Summative assessment is the assessment *of* learning.
Why?	Checks learning to determine what to do next and then provides suggestions on what to do. Is designed to assist educators and students in improving learning.	Checks what has been learned at specific checkpoints, such as mid-term, end-of-term etc. Is designed to provide information not only to teachers and students, but also to those who are not directly involved in daily learning and teaching, such as the administration or HR, parents, National School Boards, etc.
How?	Is presented on an ongoing basis as descriptive feedback to learners. Class and term tests in schools and colleges. Examples: *Check Your Understanding* or *Knowledge Check* in online courses.	Is presented in a periodic report. Examples: End-of-year Report Card in schools; certificates in colleges and end-of-course assessments in online courses.

Table 8.1: Formative & Summative Assessment

Designing formative assessments

The primary purpose of formative assessment is to improve students' learning and teachers' teaching. Learners need opportunities at frequent intervals to ascertain where they are vis-à-vis the learning goals and what needs to be done to achieve these. A good formative assessment provides evidence, which helps teachers and trainers to take instructional decisions. In addition, it also serves as practice, and provides a road map to learners.

For formative assessment to be meaningful, you must design questions carefully. Here are some guidelines to help you design effective formative assessment.

Placement

If you present a question to check a concept soon after it is taught, you inadvertently reduce the challenge level. There is always a *recency* factor in learning – things most recently learned are best remembered. Therefore, chances that the learner will get the question right are high, and it will require less cognitive effort to recall the information. This could develop a false sense of confidence in learners and negate the impact of retrieval practice.

Challenge

The more effort a learner makes in retrieving the information, the more effective the learning is. When we design online learning, we create objective type questions, and that too mostly **Multiple-Choice Questions** (**MCQ**). Fill-in-the-blank (for objective questions) and short-answer questions are better choices for formative assessments. Remember, formative assessment is the evaluation *for* learning, which means that you do not have to score the learner, so these question types can be easily added. Such questions require the learner to *supply* the answer as against *recognizing* the answer from a list of options and have proven to be more effective than simple recognition tests.

Feedback

Feedback is a great tool to teach through formative assessment. Use it as a mechanism to reinforce learning. If the learner gets the answer to a question wrong, provide feedback that will rectify the understanding or lead the learner to revisit the concept. If the content is open-ended (doesn't have a single correct answer), provide *expert views*, so that the learner can compare his/her response to the expert's opinion.

Summative assessment/evaluation

As mentioned earlier, creating a good assessment is both art and science. You may develop the art over a period of time through practice. However, a lack of understanding of the science can render your most sincere artwork ineffective. So, what are the *scientific aspects* of assessment design that teachers, trainers, and instructional designers must keep in mind when they design summative assessment/evaluation? Well there are four, as explained in the following section.

Reliability

Reliability is the term used to describe the fact that a test measures what it claims to measure consistently. Simply put, if the same candidate took the test again (a day, week, or month later), they would get a test score similar to what they scored in the first attempt. The purpose of the reliability measure is to ensure that the test produces consistent information. Reliability is represented as "r", which is the correlation between scores at Time 1 and Time 2. "r" is expressed as a number between 0 and 1.00, as follows:

- r = 0, indicates no reliability
- r = 1.00 indicates perfect reliability

Note: A test is considered reliable if it has a greater reliability coefficient. However, no test has the perfect reliability (1.00).

Validity

Validity is defined as the extent to which scores obtained on a test represents what it *claims* to measure. In other words, a test full of recall-level questions aimed at measuring the learning outcome *"apply instructional design principles"* is NOT a valid test. Or, if the objective of a learning program is to skill people to interpret and extrapolate Bloom's Taxonomy or Gagne's Events, then testing them on recalling the levels in Bloom's Taxonomy and events in Gagne's Events is again NOT a valid test. So, basically, a valid test is one that is relevant to, and measures directly what it claims to measure, which is the learning outcome.

Tip: Validity will tell you how effective a test is for a stated context; reliability will tell you how trustworthy a score on that test will be.

Difficulty index

Difficulty index is used to describe how effectively a test differentiates between candidates who do well on the test and those who don't. You arrive at this index by dividing the number of students who choose the correct answer for a test item by the number of total students. A test item is considered easy if it has a value of 0.75 or more; and difficult if it has a value of 0.25 or less.

$$\frac{\text{Number of students who select the correct answer}}{\text{Total number of students}}$$

Discrimination index

Discrimination index is the term used to describe how well an assessment differentiates between high and low scorers. A good test is one in which the high-performing candidates would select the correct answer for each question more often than the low-performing candidates. To calculate this, you first create a table of high scorers and low scorers for a test item. And suppose, eight students in the higher-scoring group answered the question correctly, and eight students in the lower-scoring group also answered the same question correctly, it means that that the test item is not very discriminatory.

> **Note: A high discrimination index is what a good test must strive to achieve. Test items with negative discrimination index must be analyzed thoroughly, and corrected or replaced.**

Assessing declarative knowledge

Recall the two types of knowledge (declarative and procedural) that we addressed in *Chapter 3, Designing the Outline*? And the three domains of learning (cognitive, affective and psychomotor) that we covered in *Chapter 4, Defining Learning Outcomes*? Assessment is directly linked to both these concepts, and the assessment tools that you deploy will depend upon the type of knowledge, and/or the domain being tested.

Declarative knowledge refers to facts, concepts, and principles that need to be known and/or understood to accomplish a task or to solve a problem. These can be in the cognitive, psychomotor, or affective domains. If the learning outcome for a training program on storyboarding is to write a storyboard, you may want learners to know and understand various frameworks, such as Gagne's Events or Bloom's Taxonomy. This is declarative knowledge and can be assessed using objective-type questions in online learning.

Objective questions are easy to administer and evaluate online. They also ensure uniformity in scoring. Declarative knowledge can also be evaluated through subjective or open-ended questions, such as essay, critique, discussion, and experiments. However, such questions are not easy to administer and evaluate online.

Multiple choice questions (MCQ)

An MCQ consists of two parts – the stem and the list of suggested solutions or alternatives. The stem may be in the form of either a question or an incomplete statement, and the list of alternatives contains one correct or best alternative (answer) and a number of incorrect or inferior alternatives (distracters). It is not easy to create challenging MCQs. This is especially true for instructional designers, most of whom may not possess subject knowledge. Hence, it is necessary that they collaborate with subject matter experts when they create questions.

Keep the following guidelines in mind when designing MCQs:

- Avoid the use of words such as *never, always,* and *only*. These words are included in distracters to make them false, but they serve as flags to the alert learner.
- Do not use keywords in the alternatives or stem. When a word or phrase in the stem is also found in one of the alternatives, it tips the learner off that the alternative is probably the answer.
- In general, avoid the alternatives "all of the above" and "none of the above".
- Make sure that all options – correct answer and distracters – are parallel in length.
- If you use a negative word in the question stem, highlight the word.

The following is an example of an MCQ:

Example 8.1: Multiple choice question

Which one of the following reflects a Behaviorist principle?

a) Your manager designs a job-aid with a mnemonic to help you recall the steps for entering data into the effort tracking system.

b) An organization delays crediting the monthly salary if the employee doesn't attend a scheduled training.

c) An expert assigns your team a project to identify ways of improving productivity at your workplace.

Correct answer: **b**

Multi-select questions (MMCQ)

Multi-select questions, also known as **multiple-multiple choice questions (MMCQ)**, allow learners to make more than one selection from a set of possible answers. The following is an example of a multi-select question:

Example 8.2: Multiple-multiple choice question

Which of the following objectives are at a level higher than recall? Select the correct options.

a) List the various frameworks for writing objectives.

b) Script a topic by applying Gagne's framework.

c) Identify the guidelines for scripting.

d) Illustrate with examples, the cognitive theory of learning.

Correct answer: **b, d**

Fill in the blank

In a **Fill-in-the-blank** type of question, the learner is asked to respond with a word, phrase, or name. It is more challenging than MCQs when designed well. They are also good question types if some terms and jargon related to a concept need to be recalled or understood. When learners attempt to fill in a blank, they try to *retrieve* information without seeing any options. This requires more effort than *recognizing* the correct answer from a list of options. This is known as **effortful retrieval**, and helps learners to transfer information to the long-term memory. The following is an example of this type of question:

Example 8.3: Fill-in-the-blank

The three domains of learning are cognitive, affective, and _____.

Correct answer: **Psychomotor**

Matching questions

Matching test items consist of a column of premises, a column of responses, and directions for matching the two. Matching test items, like multiple-choice, are selection items. They are specialized for use when measuring the learner's ability to identify the relationship between a set of similar items, each of which has two components. For example, words and their definitions, symbols and their meanings, dates and events, people and their accomplishments, and so on. The following example depicts a matching type of question:

Example 8.4: Matching question

Listed here are the three learning theories. Match the theory in Column A with the examples in Column B.

Column A	Column B
Constructivist	A badge for securing 90% in an online course
Behaviorist	Create a mental schema
Cognitive	Group discussion on a topic

Correct answer: **1-C; 2-A; 3-B**

Subjective questions

Subjective questions are considered more challenging since the learner is expected to supply a detailed answer, as against recognizing the answer from a list of options. Let's continue with the same example that we used for objective-type questions, and see how a subjective question for the same can be designed. The following is an example of a long-answer type of question:

Example 8.5: Long-answer type

Explain when and why you would recommend using Gagne's framework to design a unit of instruction. Illustrate using examples.

Subjective questions are difficult to administer and evaluate. As of now, long-answer question types cannot be evaluated automatically in online learning. Learners will need to upload their responses through the LMS, or email it to teachers and facilitators.

> Note: You can have three options in an MCQ, and not necessarily four. As per latest research, MCQ items with three-response options (one correct answer with two distracters) is comparable to, and possibly preferable over, traditional MCQ item formats consisting of four or five-response options.

Assessing procedural knowledge

Procedural knowledge addresses how to do something, such as solve a problem or perform a task. It is the *ability to work* or *produce a tangible work output* by applying cognitive, affective, or psychomotor skills. Therefore, it involves both covert (cognitive) and overt (physical or behavioral, and hence visible) procedures. This is best assessed by allowing learners to perform the task in realistic or simulated settings. However, learners must be provided with the requisite tools and equipment needed to complete the task. In addition, relevant performance parameters, such as productivity, quality, and speed must be shared with the learners, and the examiners must assess students on these parameters.

While hard skills for a profession are fairly easier to assess, soft-skills are a definite challenge. Habits are cultivated, and modifying habits is pretty hard. It cannot be achieved through a one-hour session or even a one-day training program. It has to be acquired over a period of time by reinforcing acceptable behaviors and penalizing unacceptable behaviors.

Table 8.2 depicts some strategies that you can use to assess procedural knowledge:

Domain	How to Assess
Cognitive	• Portfolios • Journals • Work Products
Affective	• Mock Situations • Role-plays • Observation over a period of time
Psychomotor	• Work Products • Portfolios

Table 8.2: Strategies to assess procedural knowledge

Assessing procedural knowledge can become subjective if there aren't any established parameters against which learner performance is evaluated. There are many assessment tools that we can use for this purpose.

Assessment tools

Checklists, rating scales, anecdotal records, and rubrics are assessment tools that trainers and facilitators can use to assess procedural knowledge. These tools help examiners to make an objective assessment of learner performance, vis-à-vis the key learning outcomes.

Rating scales

Unlike checklists, rating scales are non-binary. This tool allows trainers to indicate the *degree, quality,* or *frequency* of behaviors, skills, and knowledge displayed by the learner. Rating scales include the performance criteria and provide three to four responses against each of these. Let's look at an example of how and when a rating scale is useful. Suppose we have learners appearing for the same test or assessment, and we want to evaluate them based on certain fixed parameters, it is best to use the rating scale. This tool helps you to objectively evaluate work outputs, vis-à-vis various parameters.

The following is an example of a rating scale used to assess the storyboarding skills of instructional designers:

Example 8.6: Rating scale for assessing storyboarding skills of participants in a Basic ID training program

Parameter	Rating Scale			
	1: Poor	2: Satisfactory	3: Good	4: Excellent
Application of ID principles				
Ability to comprehend content				
Use of storyboard format				
Language & grammar				

Checklists

Checklists may be used to record observations of learners as they solve problems, complete tasks, or interact with peers in different learning situations. Checklists are useful for assessing procedures that have several tasks, which must be recalled and/or performed in a sequence, so that the tasks become a habit and are not skipped.

If we were to convert the rating scale into a checklist, how would that be? For each person, we would have to *check* the parameters based on their individual performances. However, in this case, the rating would be binary – either yes or no. Let's continue with our previous example of assessing storyboarding skills. The following example shows a sample checklist used to evaluate storyboarding skills:

Example 8.7: Checklist for assessing storyboarding skills of participants in a Basic ID training program

Parameter	Yes	No
Application of instructional design principles	☐	☐
Understanding of instructional writing basics	☐	☐
Ability to comprehend content	☐	☐
Correct use of storyboard format	☐	☐
Correct usage of grammar and language in the given context	☐	☐
Attention to detail	☐	☐
Focus on editorial and standards issues	☐	☐

The problem with using a checklist here is that even if the learner has 50% or 75% understanding, the trainer has to either tick or not tick. Or, the parameters have to be defined in such a manner that the percentages are captured. This tool can only assess the *minimum standard* and not *proficiency*.

Rubrics

Rubrics are also non-binary checklists. Just like rating scales, rubrics also include performance criteria and response selections. However, the responses include detailed descriptions, which are meant to help trainers to objectively assess a learner. Rubrics may be used for evaluating both processes and work products. For example, it may be used to assess a learner in the process of doing something, like using a carpentry tool or debating on a topic. Or, it may be used to assess a work product such as a wooden chair or a balance sheet. The following example provides descriptors for one parameter in evaluating storyboarding skills:

Example 8.8: Rubric for assessing storyboarding skills of participants in a Basic ID training program

Parameter	1	2	3	4
Application of instructional design principles	Is not able to apply basic ID principles.	Is able to apply standard ID principles, such as objective-writing and gaining attention.	Is able to make value judgments and apply ID principles that are relevant in the stated context.	Is able to make value judgments and apply ID principles that are relevant in the stated context in a creative way.

Anecdotal notes

Anecdotal notes are used to record specific observations of learner behaviors, skills, and attitudes. They are records maintained on an on-going basis by trainers who observe students performing a task or interacting with peers in the classroom. This tool is effective for assessing soft skills or skills in the affective domain.

Evaluating workplace training

So far, we addressed assessments that are created and administered as part of a lesson or after completing a course. The purpose of such assessment is to test learner understanding and/or learner capabilities. These assessments are mapped to the learning outcomes of an online module, a classroom course, or a training program.

In corporate organizations, there is another evaluation that takes place. This involves measuring the effectiveness of the training itself. The purpose of such evaluation is to determine whether the training intervention actually helped the organization in any way. For instance, did employee productivity increase? Or, did the quality of a work product increase?

Kirkpatrick model

Donald Kirkpatrick, Professor Emeritus at the University of Wisconsin and past president of the **American Society for Training and Development (ASTD)**, came up with a Four-Level Training Evaluation Model for measuring training effectiveness in organizations. This model was first published in 1959, in the US Training and Development Journal.

Table 8.3 presents the four levels and a description of what is measured at each level:

Level	What is measured
1: Learner Reaction	This level measures how trainees (the people being trained), reacted to the overall training. This is collated through Training Feedback forms. *Example: Overall rating of 3.5 out of 5 on a training program.*
2: Learning	This level measures what trainees have learned. How much has their knowledge increased as a result of the training? This is determined through summative assessment (evaluation) scores. *Example: Summative assessment at the end of a program/course*
3: Learner Behavior	This level measures how much the trainees have changed their behavior, or how they are performing after the training. Specifically, this looks at how trainees apply what they learned in workplace situations. This is ascertained through Employee Performance Appraisals. *Example: Demonstrate time management skills at work*
4: Program Results	This level measures the final results of training. This includes outcomes that the organization has determined to be good for business, good for the employees, or good for the bottom line. This is measured through return on investment(ROI). *Example: Increased productivity by 10% in 6 months*

Table 8.3: Kirkpatrick's Model of Evaluation

Challenges in measuring training ROI

As you can see in *Table 8.3*, the Kirkpatrick Model includes an evaluation of ROI. Corporate organizations exist in order to make profits. Hence, this element is included in the overall training evaluation. However, determining Training ROI is not easy for various reasons. Firstly, organizations are rarely static. There's always something happening – a new boss, changes in team configurations, change in processes, and introduction of new software, to name a few. It is difficult to isolate the training factor – in other words, how much did training contribute to the business result (such as reduction in rework, increase in productivity, or customer satisfaction). Secondly, determining ROI involves effort, and most times, the effort is spread over a long period and involves more than one department (HR, L&D, Administration, Operations, and Senior Management). This will cost the organization money. Finally, training results in certain benefits that cannot be measured easily. For example, training can result in improving employee morale, better teamwork, and lesser conflicts, increased commitment to the organization, and reduced complaints. This is soft data, or intangibles, which cannot be assigned a monetary value.

Conclusion

In this chapter, we looked at the *Evaluation* phase of the ADDIE model, which deals with the various modes in which learning is assessed. We addressed the differences between formative and summative assessments, and looked at objective and subjective question types. We also learned how to assess declarative knowledge and the assessment tools that can be used to assess procedural knowledge.

In the next chapter, we will go through a few case studies that will depict how instructional design principles are applied in different contexts.

Points to remember

- Evaluation is the final phase in the ADDIE model and involves assessing learner performance and evaluation of the training process itself.

- Learner performance is assessed both during the learning process and after the learning process. Assessment that forms part of the learning process is known as formative assessment. Assessment administered to judge participant performance after the learning process is called summative assessment.

- Formative assessment is the assessment *for* learning, while summative assessment or evaluation is the assessment *of* learning.

- Assessments may be designed as objective questions. These are easy to administer and evaluate online.

- Some cognitive tasks that require learners to supply a detailed answer may be assessed with the help of subjective or open-ended questions, such as essays and critique.

- In the workplace, the work process or work output needs to be assessed. Assessment tools, such as checklists, rating scales, anecdotal records, and rubrics help in such assessment.

- In corporate organizations, the Kirkpatrick model of evaluation is used. This evaluates the learners and the learning process across four levels – learner reaction, learning, transfer of learning, and return on investment.

Multiple Choice Questions

1. Which of the following statements best describes summative assessment?

    a) It is the assessment *for* learning.

    b) It helps teachers and students to improve learning.

    c) It is administered to generate a report of pass/fail.

2. Which of the following is the best way to assess a task with the following attributes: a) it doesn't call for proficiency; b) it includes a number of sub-tasks, and c) completing every sub-task is significant?

    a) Checklists

    b) Written exam

    c) Rubric

    d) Rating scale

3. The difficulty index of a test item is 0.85. What does this mean?

    a) It is easy

    b) It is tough

    c) It is unreliable

    d) It is not valid

4. _____ is the term used to describe whether a test assesses the outcomes that it is intended to measure.

    a) Reliability

    b) Validity

    c) Discrimination index

    d) Difficulty index

5. **Identify the attribute of objective-type questions.**

    a) It is comprehensive

    b) Response to questions may vary

    c) There is uniformity in scoring

Answers

1. c
2. a
3. a
4. b
5. c

Questions

1. Describe the *evaluate* phase of the ADDIE model.
2. Distinguish between formative and summative assessments.
3. List the guidelines to be followed when creating multiple choice questions (MCQs).
4. Why is Fill-in-the-blank a better objective-type question than a multiple-choice question?
5. Explain the Kirkpatrick model of evaluation.

Key terms

- *Evaluation:* The final phase in the ADDIE model in which learner performance and instructional effectiveness are evaluated.

- *Formative assessment:* Questions that form a part of the learning process and provides learners with a road map, and teachers/trainers with information for improving the learning process.

- *Summative assessment:* It is the assessment *of* learning presented as a periodic report to teachers, learners, and other stakeholders.

- *Objective questions:* These are fixed-response questions, where a respondent's answer can be determined as right or wrong.

- *Subjective questions:* These are varied-response questions, where a respondent's answer is given a grade or score based on the examiner's evaluation.

- *Test validity:* Validity is defined as the extent to which scores obtained on a test represents what it *claims* to measure.

- *Test reliability:* It is the term used to describe the fact that a test measures what it claims to measure consistently.

- *Difficulty index:* This term is used to describe how effectively a test differentiates between candidates who do well on the test and those who don't.

- *Discrimination index:* This term is used to describe how well an assessment differentiates between high and low scorers.

- *Rating scale:* It is a tool that allows trainers to indicate the *degree, quality,* or *frequency* of behaviors, skills, and knowledge displayed by the learner.

- *Checklists:* This is an assessment tool used to assess procedures that have several tasks, which must be recalled and/or performed in a sequence.

- *Rubrics:* This is an assessment tool which includes performance criteria and detailed descriptions of the various parameters on which a learner is assessed.

- *Anecdotal notes:* This is an assessment tool that is used to record specific observations of learner behaviors, skills, and attitudes over a period of time.

CHAPTER 9
Case Studies

The academic world is ideal; the workplace, messy. The former gives you knowledge; the latter, experience. One tests what you know and understand; the other assesses your productivity and efficiency. To be effective as an instructional designer, you must have a thorough understanding of learning science and the content development process. We addressed both these areas in the preceding chapters.

However, knowledge and understanding is not enough to work as an instructional designer. The project requirements vary in the workplace, and instructional designers are expected to be creative within these requirements. In other words, there are always "buts" and "however", which must be considered when executing a project. Let's consider a few examples:

Example 9.1:

"We want an effective program. The trainees should be able to improve their productivity and product quality after the training. But, we have only a limited budget."

"Our math product must be unique. It should be completely different from the ones that are currently available in the market. However, we need to hit the road running."

"The sales team should be able to achieve higher targets after the training. But, they cannot take time away from work to attend the training."

As you can see, in the real-world, we need to make judgment calls, take decisions, and consider a trade-off. This is in sharp contrast to an ideal world, where we assume we can adopt the most effective approach to designing a training program, a course, or a learning product. In this chapter, we will look at how instructional design decisions are made and analyze a few case studies.

Structure

In this chapter, we will discuss the following topics:

- Factors that impact decision-making in instructional design
- Case studies in instructional design

Objectives

After studying this chapter, you will be able to describe the factors that impact the decision-making process in instructional design. In addition, you will go through four case studies which will detail the instructional approach adopted to meet the needs of the situation, and the rationale for selecting the specific approach. The case studies will address the following domains– K-12, higher education, corporate training, and vocational skills.

Introduction

In the real world, apart from the three variables – audience, content, and learning outcome – there are other factors that impact design decisions. These factors must also be considered to determine the instructional strategy for a given context. We saw that defining the strategy is not a simple linear process, but involves complex decision-making. So, then what is the common trade-off involved in making instructional design decisions? There could be many, and it depends upon the context. But, by and large, we can identify two main factors that impacts instructional design decisions – time and budget or cost.

Engagement versus time/cost

Very often training and product budgets pose constraints. We may think that a game-based approach will work in a given situation; and the client may request for the same too. But a real game that teaches something and makes the content engaging takes time and effort, and requires senior resources from instructional design, technology, and media to collaborate. This has an impact on both time and cost. If you don't consider this at project start, you may end up making a game that doesn't teach, but is just a wrapper to the content. If budget is a constraint, you may decide to use a strategy less impactful than gamification for learner engagement.

Effectiveness versus time/cost

Online training, when deployed properly, can help learners to learn anytime from anywhere. This can cut down the logistical requirements that come with hands-on or field training, and can save time and money. But, at the same time, this may impact the training effectiveness in some situations – for example, if online training is considered for military personnel, it could reduce the military personnel's confidence in the use of real warfare equipment. In this situation, you may consider effectiveness over cost.

One-time investment versus recurring costs

Typically, online learning is seen as a one-time investment. In most cases, it would be so. But there are situations where the content is frequently updated. This happens in evolving fields, such as technology. For instance, there is a lot of buzz around **Artificial Intelligence (AI)** these days, and almost every company/institution is creating a course on the subject. However, the field is still evolving, which means that the content could change. When designing online training, you must consider how to structure it, so that updating is easy. Here is another situation. You may consider virtual reality (VR) as the best way to train people in a certain context. But while doing so, you must take note of the expense involved, if this has to be scaled across the organization. The headsets used in VR are evolving quickly, and what you purchase today may soon become outdated.

Figure 9.1 depicts the process of arriving at instructional design decisions:

Figure 9.1: *Decision-making in instructional design projects*

To sum up, arriving at a design decision is a complex process. First and foremost, we must consider the three variables – audience, content, and learning outcome. When we do so, we may come up with the ideal pedagogy, strategy, and delivery media to design the material. While we may want to design and deploy the most engaging and effective solution, we must also be cognizant of the fact that, in the real world, there is a trade-off involved, and we have to strike a fine balance between learner engagement, learning effectiveness, and development costs. In the following section, we will analyze a few case studies that will help us see how instructional design is applied in the workplace.

Case study 1 – Mathematics anxiety

Securing at least a grade 4 in GCSE English and Mathematics is an important qualification to have in the UK in order to get a job. Certain educational courses also have this as admission criteria, even if the educational course is completely unrelated to Mathematics. Those who achieved a grade less than 4 have to reattempt the exam to gain their qualification in these two subjects. This case study involves a product designed to help students who have to reattempt the GCSE exam in Mathematics. Such students are prone to Mathematics anxiety, and the solution had to take this into account.

> **Note:** "More detailed investigation in 1,700 UK schoolchildren found that a general feeling that Maths was more difficult than other subjects often contributed to Maths anxiety, leading to a lack or loss of confidence. Students pointed to poor marks or test results, or negative comparisons to peers or siblings as reasons for feeling anxious."
>
> Source:https://www.cam.ac.uk/research/news/report-examines-origins-and-nature-of-maths-anxiety, retrieved 28 November, 2021

Background

As we saw through the various chapters in this book, instructional design has three variables – the audience, the content, and the learning outcome. *Table 9.1* details the three variables in this case study:

Variable	Details
Audience	Students who have to reattempt the GCSE exam
	Students with Mathematics anxiety
Content	Foundation Mathematics: Numbers, Algebra, Geometry, Proportion & Statistics
Learning Outcome	Achieve a minimum of Grade 4

Table 9.1: Case study 1 variables

Mathematics is considered a tough subject to master by many students. Why is it so? Let's see with the help of an analogy.

Suppose you are playing a game that involves a treasure hunt. You have to solve a series of puzzles, and for every puzzle that you solve, you get a clue that leads you closer to the treasure. If you don't solve one, then you cannot move to the next puzzle, and as a consequence, you don't reach the treasure. Mathematics is something like that. Every new concept builds on what you already know and understand. So, somewhere along the way, if a student fails to master a concept, then they fall behind. Recall, in *Chapter 3, Designing the Outline,* we had addressed the concept of element interactivity. Mathematics is a subject with high element interactivity. In the book, *Mind, Brain and Education – Neuroscience Implications for Classroom*, which is a compilation of studies in neuroscience and teaching, author Dr. Keith Devlin, in the chapter, *The Mathematical Brain* has the following to say about learning Mathematics:

"Our brains are not at all suited to the kinds of precise manipulations of information that arise in Arithmetic – they did not evolve to do Arithmetic. To do Arithmetic, we have to marshal mental circuits that developed (or were selected during evolution) for quite different reasons. It's like using the edge of a small coin to turn a screw. Sure, you can do it, but it's slow, and the outcome is not always perfect."

So, it is no surprise that many students experience anxiety when they are learning Mathematics or solving Mathematical problems. As it is, Mathematics places a load on working memory, and anxiety adds to the load, which further impacts student performance. In addition, Mathematics material and teachers regardless of grade, mostly adopt the *procedural fluency* approach in teaching the subject. This involves demonstrating specific procedures to students and then supplementing this with practice exercises. It's a *"one-size-fits-all"* type of approach. Clearly, this strategy didn't work for the target audience, which is why they have to reattempt the GCSE examination.

> **Note:** A key insight from the analysis phase was that this is a group of learners who have not had a positive experience with learning Mathematics in school. They needed patient tutoring, lots of practice, and varied teaching strategies, and not just the procedural fluency approach.

Solution – Adaptive approach

Benjamin Bloom, in a paper titled the *2 Sigma Problem,* in 1984 compared three modes of teaching – lecture, lecture with feedback, and one-to-one tuition. He found an 84% increase in mastery for the lecture with feedback approach and 98% mastery for one-to-one tuition. The instructional design approach adopted to address this learning need was to leverage media and technology to develop a self-paced learning product that would be similar to a personal tutor.

The product design was also influenced by the *Lesh Translation Model*, which comprises five different ways of representing Mathematics – using manipulatives, picture representations, real-life contexts, and verbal and written symbols. Manipulatives are objects that students can touch and move around, such as an abacus. Since this solution was technology-driven, virtual manipulatives were included.

Refer to *Figure 9.2* that depicts the LESH Translation model:

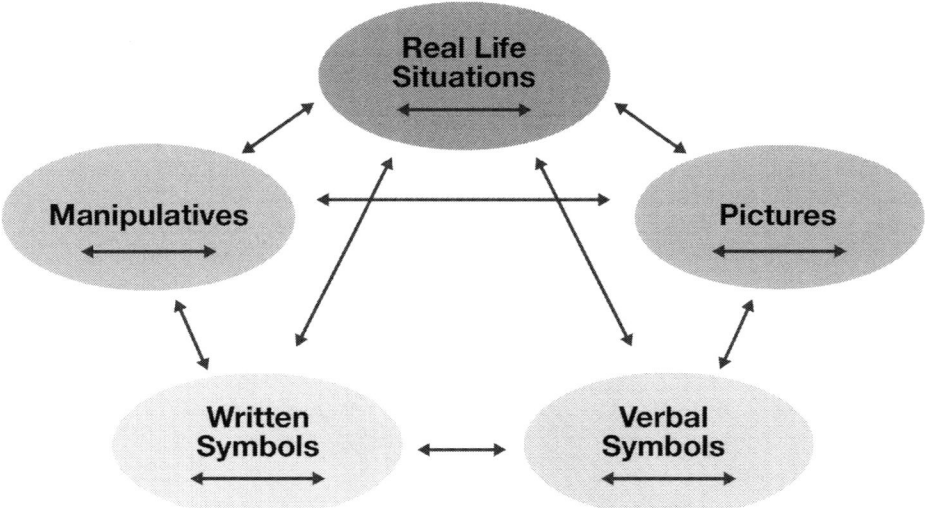

Figure 9.2: LESH Translation model

Personal tutoring

The solution adopts a problem-based approach and works as follows –when the learner logs into the system the first time, they have to attempt a pre-assessment. This includes a number of questions ranging from easy to difficult and covering all the foundational concepts. The system evaluates the learner and identifies the concepts which need to be revised. The learner then selects a concept to practice. A question is posed and if the learner gets it right, the system presents a more difficult question. If the learner gets the answer wrong, they receive feedback from the system which works as a sort of hint to help the learner solve the question. After three wrong attempts, the system displays the correct response and prompts the learner to go through the video tutorial, which explains the concept. Refer to *Figure 9.3* that depicts the approach to product design:

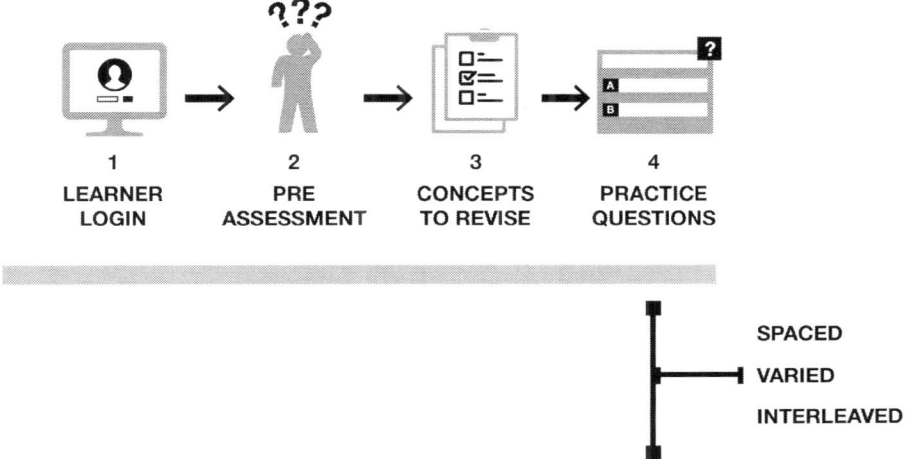

Figure 9.3: Approach to product design

Exercise design

The practice questions are designed keeping in mind the following guidelines:

- **Spaced practice:** The system registers the time spent by a learner and alerts them to take a break from the concept after a few minutes. This is known as spaced practice, which is a learning technique of revisiting a concept after a time gap. The time gap makes learners forget, and the next time they revisit the concept, they have to make an extra effort to retrieve the information. Effortful retrieval helps to store information in long-term memory.

- **Interleaved practice:** The system shuffles the practice questions. For example, if a learner has attempted problems relating to percentages, then the next set of questions that are posed are related to a different concept, such as fractions or decimals. This is known as interleaving, which is another proven technique for registering information in the long-term memory.

- **Varied practice:** The same problem is rendered in different ways. Some are presented using visuals, such as a number line or a grid, while some are presented in the form of real-world tasks. Constantly confronting different manifestations of the same problem ensures that students understand the underlying principles, and not just memorize the procedure to solve a problem.

As displayed in *Figure 9.4*, the problems get progressively complex across two dimensions:

- Complex in terms of the content; represented as *numbers* in the columns and,
- Complex in terms of how the problem is designed; whether visually, verbally, using a real-life context, and so on. This is represented as *letters* across rows

Refer to *Figure 9.4* that depicts the approach to question design:

	Problem-design complexity					
Content complexity	Q1a	Q1b	Q1c	Q1d	Q1e	Q1f
	Q2a	Q2b	Q2c	Q2d	Q2e	Q2f
	Q3a	Q3b	Q3c	Q3d	Q3e	Q3f
	Q4a	Q4b	Q4c	Q4d	Q4e	Q4f
	Q5a	Q5b	Q5c	Q5d	Q5e	Q5f
	Q6a	Q6b	Q6c	Q6d	Q6e	Q6f
	Video explanation of the concept (if required)					

Figure 9.4: Approach to question design

The following example illustrates a simple problem on the concept of percentage depicted visually using a grid. Notice, how feedback for incorrect responses work as hints to lead the learner to the correct answer:

Example 9.2

Here is a square grid. Shade the grid as specified. Select the drop-down arrow against a color and then select the total number of squares to match with the percentage.

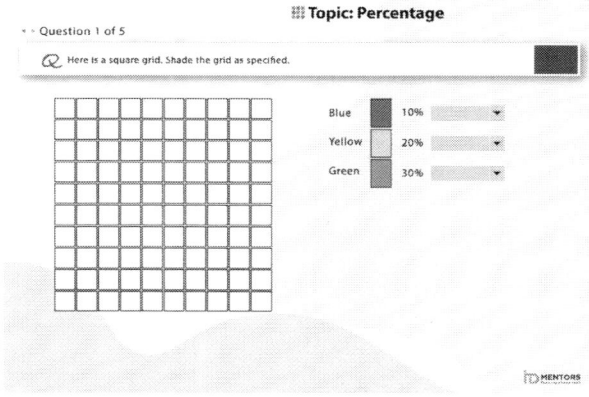

Figure 9.5: Square grid

Correct Feedback

Well done!

Incorrect Feedback (1)

10% means 10 divided by hundred and then multiplied by the absolute value. Why don't you try again?

Incorrect Feedback (2)

The absolute value here is 100. Why don't you try again?

Incorrect Feedback (3)

1% means 1 square out of 100, so what would 10%, 20%, and 30% mean? Why don't you try again?

After 3 wrong attempts

The correct values are displayed. Mistakes are part of the learning process. Keep trying with the aim to get the next question right.

The following example illustrates a more difficult problem on the concept of percentage depicted visually:

Example 9.3

Here is a representation of a football field. The entire field is made up of 240 squares. Calculate the percentage taken up by the penalty area.

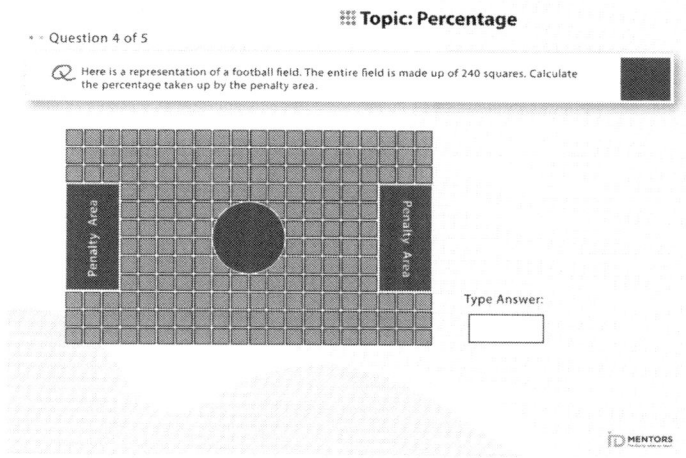

Correct Feedback

Well done!

Incorrect Feedback

Percentage is the proportion in relation to the whole. How many colored squares are there in the Penalty area? Why don't you try again?

Incorrect Feedback

Percentage is the proportion in relation to the whole. The whole here is 240. Why don't you try again?

Incorrect Feedback

The proportion is the total number of squares in the two penalty areas, and the whole is 240 as stated in the problem. Why don't you try again?

After 3 wrong attempts

The correct values are displayed. Mistakes are part of the learning process. Keep trying with the aim to get the next question right.

The following example presents a percentage problem framed using a real-world context. In addition, it provides a visual tool in the form of a number line to help learners visualize and solve the problem:

Example 9.4

Suppose you opt for trim and color with the special offer. How much will you pay?

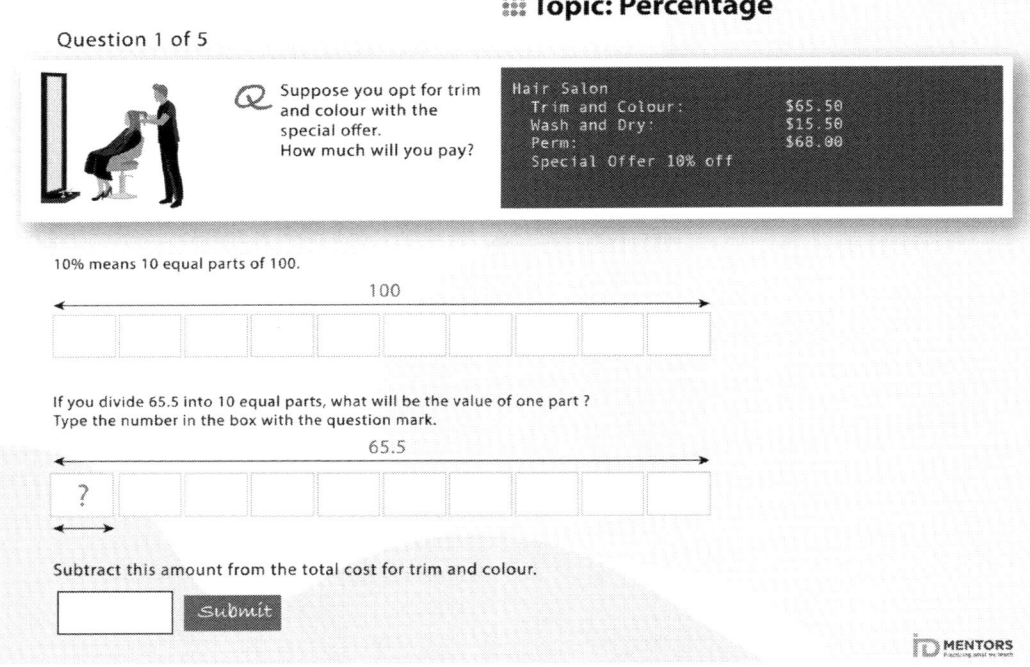

Subtract this amount from the total cost for trim and color.

Correct

Well done!

Incorrect attempt 1:

A percentage problem involves finding out any one of the following: the missing part, the missing percentage, or the whole. Which is the missing part in this problem? Why don't you try again?

Incorrect attempt 2:

The percentage is given (10%); and the whole is given (65.5). You have to find the missing part. Why don't you try again?

Incorrect attempt 3:

Since the percentage value is 10%, you will need to divide 65.5 in the second bar into 10 equal parts. This will give you the value of the missing part. Why don't you try again?

After 3 wrong attempts

The correct values are displayed. Mistakes are part of the learning process. Keep trying with the aim to get the next question right.

Case study 2–Entrepreneurship orientation program

Consider a hypothetical scenario. Suppose, you are passionate about cooking, and you start a small café in a cottage that you inherit. The café is near a college and you offer a variety of snacks, coffee, and tea to customers. So far, you have managed the café with your friend. But soon you find the café hustling and bustling with customers, most of whom are from the colleges nearby. You realize that you need more hands to handle the increasing business. In addition, your chartered accountant tells you that there are some regulatory issues that your business must comply with. Now, you suddenly find yourself interacting with government institutions, and running around to register and legitimize your business. This takes you away from the café and your friend is unable to manage the customers by himself, and the customers start complaining. That's when the realization dawns! Entrepreneurship gives you freedom to pursue your passion, but it also comes with a number of challenges. Now you wish you had considered and addressed these challenges prior to starting the café.

Entrepreneurship is an emerging trend in India. The success of many young entrepreneurs, such as Ritesh Agarwal (of OYO rooms), Farrhad Acidwalla (of Rockstah Media), and King Siddharth (of the online magazine Friendz) have contributed to making the Indian youth aware of self-employment and entrepreneurship as a career option.

Background

The goal of the training, *Entrepreneurship Expedition*, is to introduce the concept of entrepreneurship and self-employment to students pursuing undergraduate studies in a college based in Gujarat, India. It was designed as a two-month long summer program. An analysis of the target audience revealed that a majority of them were interested in starting a small venture right after college. However, the reasons that they gave for the same were rather utopian, built perhaps on the success stories they read and heard about young entrepreneurs. The fact that setting up and running a venture requires grit, determination, risk, hard work, patience etc., were hidden behind the veneer of entrepreneurial glamour. *Table 9.2* details the variables in this case study:

Variable	Details
Audience	Students enrolled in various undergraduate courses
Content	Entrepreneurship Orientation
Learning Outcome	Understand how to set up a small venture and experience the challenges it involves.

Table 9.2: Case Study 2 Variables

This short summer program is designed to provide the youth with a complete experience – the good and the bad – of starting a venture in simulated settings. Through this course, learners are exposed to the various aspects involved in setting up and running a business. They are guided through the various stages of a business starting from developing a business idea, to setting up the infrastructure and marketing the product or service. By the end of the training, the learners would have a sample business plan that they would pitch to angel investors.

Note: A key insight from the analysis phase was that the target audience is enamored by the glamour that comes with being a young entrepreneur and does not need any inspirational stories for motivation. What was required, rather, was a reality check, which could be achieved through experiential learning.

Solution – Task-based approach

The outline for this short summer training was designed around the key tasks involved in starting a venture. As you can observe in *Table 9.3*, each week focused on a specific task to be completed. Concepts and principles that needed to be learned and understood were dovetailed into these week-wise tasks. The students were divided into groups and each group was assigned a mentor who would advise them if they needed any support. Refer to *Table 9.3*:

Week	Stage	Activities
1	Find venture partners	<ul><li>Assess your entrepreneurial personality</li><li>Create your personal profile</li><li>Identify co-founders who will complement your style</li><li>Allocate roles, such as CEO, CFO, and Marketing & Sales etc.</li></ul>
2	Set up your venture (on paper)	<ul><li>Pick an area for your venture (software, restaurant, travel, training, and so on)</li><li>Specify the type of venture – sole proprietorship, partnership, limited liability company, corporation, and so on</li><li>Identify a name, tagline, and logo for your business</li><li>Ideate how you will brand the venture</li></ul>
3	Ascertain regulatory requirements	<ul><li>Research and look up compliance and regulatory requirements</li><li>List the regulatory tasks that must be completed to start the type of venture you have picked</li><li>Download forms and documents that are available online</li><li>Consider intellectual property rights if required</li><li>Create a folder with the requisite documentation</li></ul>

Week	Stage	Activities
4	Develop a finance and investment plan	• List capital expenses • Identify revenue and operational costs • Calculate a rough estimate of the required investment • Calculate profit • Identify sources of capital
5	Create a marketing and sales plan	• Conduct consumer analysis (segmentation and value addition) • Complete market analysis (size and growth) • Review competition & self (strengths, weakness, threats, and opportunities) • Review distribution channels (product, cash, and information) • Ascertain advertising and promotion avenues (sources, channels, target, and calendar) • Arrive at product/service pricing
6	Create a human resources allocation plan	• List key roles • Identify people with requisite skills to take up these roles
7	Develop a business plan	• Based on 1 to 6 above, create an elevator pitch for your business plan
8	Present your venture idea to mentors/angel investors	• Present your business plan to mentors and angel investors

Table 9.3: Entrepreneurial Expedition Program Outline

The instructional material developed for this training program is depicted in *Table 9.4*:

Entity	Materials
Facilitator	• Presentation slides • Facilitator handbook • Insights – video interviews of entrepreneurs • Rubrics for evaluating the business plan, and elevator pitch
Students	• Business essentials handbook • Templates and formats to complete each task

Table 9.4: Entrepreneurial Expedition – Instructional Materials

Figure 9.6 depicts the day-wise learning events in each week, which were included as part of every task:

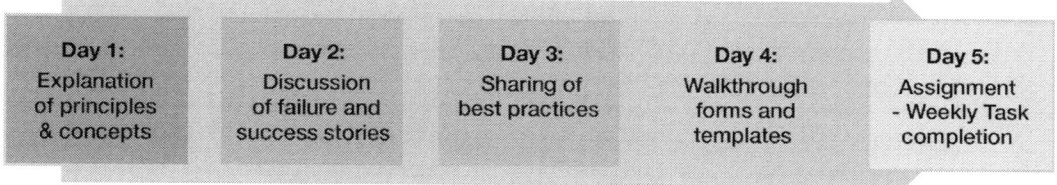

Figure 9.6: Entrepreneurial Expedition – Weekly schedule

The following example is an extract from the Entrepreneurship Essentials handbook, which includes key content and templates for student reference:

Example 9.4: An extract from the Entrepreneurship Essentials Handbook

What are the sources of capital for the investment you need?

Source	Description	Equity or Debt
Personal Money / Family and Friends		
Angels		
Seed Capital		
Venture Capital		
Banks and government programs		
Private Equity		
IPOs		

Equity financing involves the sale of some of the ownership in the venture, while the use of debt to finance a new venture involves a payback of the funds plus a fee (interest) for the use of the money.

Advantages to equity financing:

- It's less risky than a loan because you don't have to pay it back, and it's a good option if you can't afford to take on debt.
- You tap into the investor's network, which may add more credibility to your business.
- Investors take a long-term view, and most don't expect a return on their investment immediately.
- You won't have to channel profits into loan repayment.
- You'll have more cash on hand for expanding the business.
- There's no requirement to pay back the investment if the business fails.

Disadvantages to equity financing:

- It may require returns that could be more than the rate you would pay for a bank loan.
- The investor will require some ownership of your company and a percentage of the profits. You may not want to give up this kind of control.

- You will have to consult with investors before making big (or even routine) decisions -- and you may disagree with your investors.

- In the case of irreconcilable disagreements with investors, you may need to cash in your portion of the business and allow the investors to run the company without you.

- It takes time and effort to find the right investor for your company.

Advantages to debt financing:

- The bank or lending institution (such as the Small Business Administration) has no say in the way you run your company and does not have any ownership in your business.

- The business relationship ends once the money is paid back.

- The interest on the loan is tax deductible.

- Loans can be short term or long term.

- Principal and interest are known figures you can plan in a budget (provided that you don't take a variable rate loan).

Disadvantages to debt financing:

- Money must be paid back within a fixed amount of time.

- If you rely too much on debt and have cash flow problems, you will have trouble paying the loan back.

- If you carry too much debt, you will be seen as "high risk" by potential investors – which will limit your ability to raise capital by equity financing in the future.

- Debt financing can leave the business vulnerable during hard times when sales take a dip.

- Debt can make it difficult for a business to grow because of the high cost of repaying the loan.

- Assets of the business can be held as collateral to the lender. And the owner of the company is often required to personally guarantee repayment of the loan.

Case study 3 - Instructional design certification

If a company is in the business of designing multimedia material for K-12, or a publishing firm is in the business of developing academic textbooks, teachers are recruited and given a crash course in instructional design. The crash course mostly focuses on some basic instructional design theories and principles, topped with a small dose of the process involved. In current times, colleges and universities are being forced to revisit their courses and re-design them to make them blended, skill-centric, and industry-centric. So, what do these universities do? As a quick-fix approach, they may recruit people with practical experience in the industry –**Subject Matter Experts (SME)** – and get them to design or deliver courses. Then there is the final option –to outsource the design and development of learning material to EdTech companies. These companies, whose core business is to work on education and training projects, are the ones that formally recruit and train instructional designers.

Background

When companies recruit instructional designers, they check writing skills, proficiency in the English language, and basic knowledge of instructional design concepts. Most graduates with an English-medium education clear the writing skills and English language proficiency test, while the knowledge of instructional design processes and frameworks is guaranteed by a formal certificate that some of these candidates may possess – conferred upon them by one of the few formal institutes in India that offer short-term programs or certificate courses in instructional design. Many candidates successfully clear the recruitment tests, but once they get down to work, most of them fall short of meeting even the minimum expectations. Why does that happen?

A major reason for this is that the skill-set defined by most companies does not completely match with what an instructional designer is required to do at the workplace. While writing skills and proficiency in the English language are required to function effectively as an instructional designer, they are only secondary skills and *not primary skills*.

Table 9.5 depicts the key variables in this case study:

Variable	Details
Audience	Graduates and working professionals looking for or pursuing a career in instructional design
Content	Learning science, and instructional design processes, frameworks and models
Learning Outcomes	Develop instructional material for varied media and varied audience profile

Table 9.5: Case Study 3 Variables

Consider this. An instructional designer in an EdTech company is almost always expected to design learning material on a range of topics. It could be finance one month, and mining or engineering the next month. Or it could be soft-skills, information technology, and medicine and pharmacy all happening in parallel. Along with learning new content, they also need to design for different audiences, such as K-12, vocational students, college students and working professionals. The ability to write English well or the knowledge of instructional design concepts does not guarantee that the instructional designer will easily handle all kinds of content. This calls for a completely different set of skills, such as comprehension, learning, structuring, and visualizing.

> **Note:** A key insight from the analysis phase was that the focus of the training should be to develop the requisite competencies – ability to quickly comprehend information, stamina to consume volumes written by academics and SMEs, and the tenacity to keep learning new content.

Solution – Comprehensive Scaffolding Framework (CSF)©

ID Mentors, a partnership firm based in New Delhi, India, came up with a certification model called the **Comprehensive Scaffolding Framework**© to address the demand for skilled instructional designers in the country. The model identifies instructional design as the **core** of the education and training space. It is a skill that is no longer *nice-to-have*. Rather, it is a skill that will provide an edge to all knowledge givers – trainers, teachers, and subject matter experts in current times.

The CSF model incorporates the following features:

- **Comprehensive**: The model takes into account the fact that instructional design can be applied to the creation of learning materials in any delivery format and for different audiences. It is designed to give a complete view of instructional design and enable beginners and practitioners in the training and education space to move across the spectrum with confidence and ease.

- **Scaffolding**: The model recognizes instructional design as the core skill in the education and training space in current times. With that in mind, a one-stop portal has been developed to facilitate the progressive evolution of professionals in this space from a narrow understanding of instructional design to a holistic understanding of the discipline.

Figure 9.7 depicts this framework:

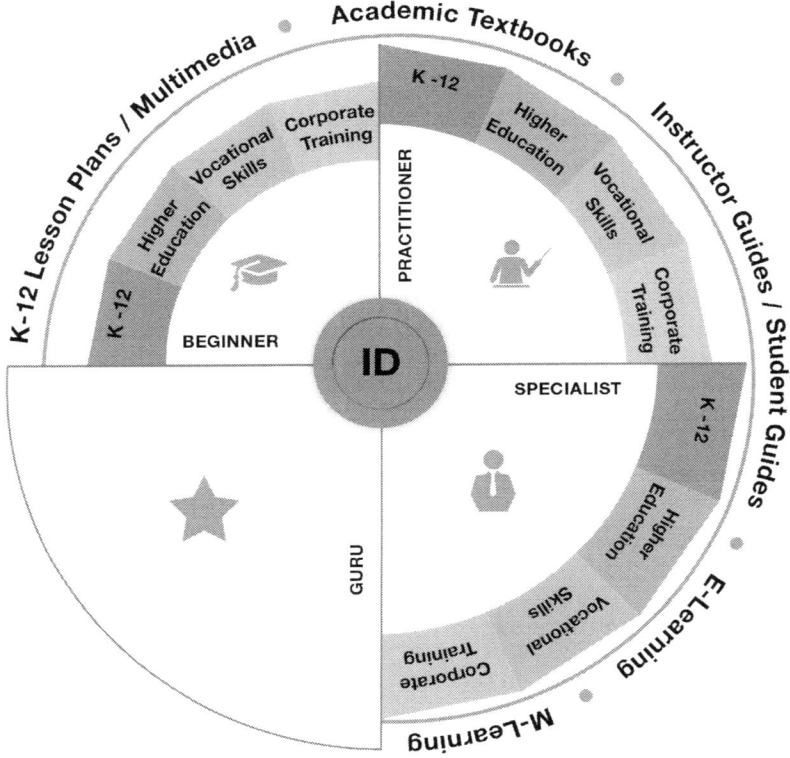

Figure 9.7: *Comprehensive Scaffolding Framework* ©

Certification levels

The certification program is designed at three levels, as described as follows:

- **Level 1 (Beginner):** At this level, established content is covered in a very structured manner. The focus is to help learners develop the skills to write content for instructional material. A structured online course is assigned and a schedule is created, which the learner is expected to follow. The learning culminates with a storyboard that is written by the learner and evaluated by the facilitator. A storyboard is usually a document with key content, audio narration, and visual and programming notes.

- **Level 2 (Intermediate):** At this level, along with established content, new trends in the field of online learning are covered. The focus at this level is the process of instructional design starting with needs assessment and culminating with training evaluation. The design of the course is semi-structured, with a lot more learner control over the learning pace. The learners have to submit a high-level design for a stated context as part of the course.

- **Level 3 (Advanced):** At this level, the evolving concepts are addressed, such as gamification, micro learning, curation, personalization, social learning, and so on. The learning pace is completely controlled by the learner, and the instructional material is not structured. Learners have to read a number of articles, explore content on their own, and write a white paper as part of the assignment. Refer to *Figure 9.8*:

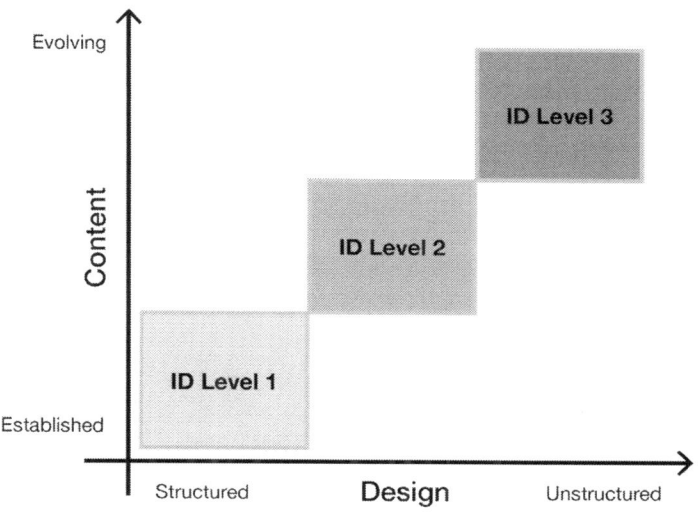

Figure 9.8: ID Certification Levels

Case study 4 – Financial inclusion program

This wasn't the regular vanilla project. The target audience wasn't school and college students or the white-collar worker with formal higher education. It was a certification program that was to be designed for rural Indian women across many states in India, a majority of whom would have at least studied up to Standard 8. They were busy homemakers, used to performing physical tasks more than mental processing. The content to be disseminated was financial concepts, something far removed from their realm of operation. And the training goal was to encourage them to adopt financial planning and become active participants in making their village financially literate.

Background

The project started with a trip to a few rural areas, to meet the target audience and gather insights about their likes, dislikes, challenges, and aspirations. What the rural women lacked in formal knowledge, they made up for it aptly with their earthy wisdom, which they had acquired through solid life experiences. *Table 9.6* depicts the variables in this case study:

Variable	Details
Audience	Rural women in Indian villages with Grade 8 as the minimum formal level of education
Content	Basic finance and banking concepts, products and procedures, and government schemes
Learning Outcomes	Certified ambassadors for promoting financial inclusion in a village

Table 9.6: Case Study 4 Variables

Meeting the target audience in rural settings challenged the stereotype that most of us have of rural Indian women, and gave ample fodder that could be used to design the certification program. In short, it would be safe to sum this up as a trip where *knowledge met wisdom.*

Note: A key insight in this context was that we need to find a common way to connect with the target audience given the cultural and regional diversity in India; help them to use technology as the learning medium and sustain the lengthy learning process.

Solution – Story-based approach

A successful and effective learning solution is one where you can take the learners from the familiar to the unfamiliar. Success of the solution also depends on how well you are able to connect the learning material with the ecosystem that the learners inhabit. Last, but not the least, learners must clearly see how spending their valuable time on something like this will benefit and change their lives for the better.

Keeping these factors in mind, a colorful fictional world was designed – one that is set in a village with a group of people having names that depicted their personality traits – *a constantly worried but talented potter, a cheerful homemaker with a talent for knitting, a happy-go-lucky peon in the local school, a cynical farmer who owns some livestock,* and so on. The character sketches were designed to ensure universal appeal – these personality traits provided the audience-connect since the project catered to a diverse audience whose appearance and attire were very different.

The main protagonist in this story is aptly named Vidya (Vidya in the Hindi language means learning), who embarks on a journey to become a certified professional in financial inclusion. She serves as the role model for these village women, who could see in her, their aspirations and the trajectory to achieve a similar position.

Every module begins with a **financial need** that one of the characters puts forth to the main protagonist, Vidya, who then explains how a financial product/service can address the need. She then walks them through the **procedure** to avail this, and also helps the character to gather and complete the necessary documentation. This strategy – starting with a financial need–would motivate the target audience and ensure they found the learning material relevant. Refer to *Figure 9.9*:

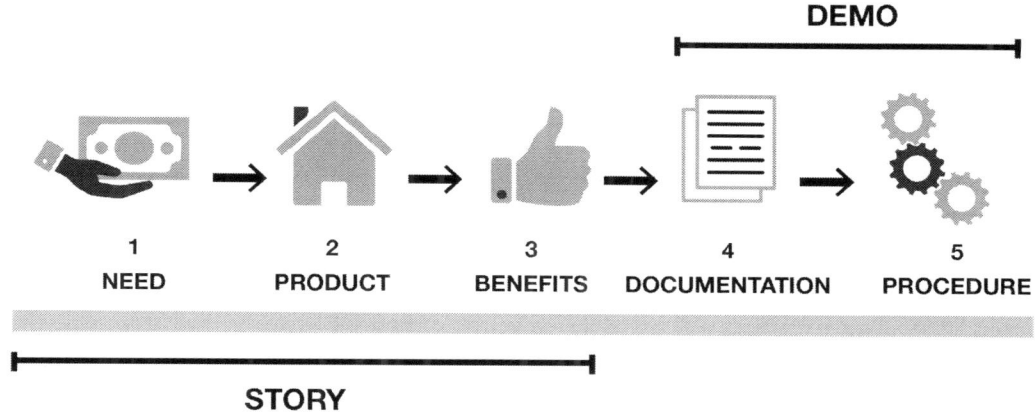

Figure 9.9: *Financial inclusion certification program – Design Approach*

The certification program is delivered through an app that is easily accessible on smart phones and tablets. The target audience is also handed a project kit that comprises of a number of financial artifacts that are a part of the course. Every village is assigned a mentor who gets the learners started with the learning program by helping them use the app to access the learning material. The mentor also periodically checks on their progress.

No learning sticks, unless the input (learning) is processed and an output is generated. Therefore, at the end of each module, the learner has to complete a real-world task, such as filling up an application form for opening a bank account, or applying for a permanent account number (PAN) card. This is uploaded to the learning portal and is checked and returned by the assigned mentor. And thus, a real-world task that is very relevant is completed by the learner.

Conclusion

Most of us understand intuitively that different content type and learning outcomes require different treatment (strategies). For example, some content may require that the learner recalls information automatically – such content is best taught using the drill and practice method. In some cases, learners require to observe fine nuances, such as body language and facial expressions – this is best addressed using role plays (either play-acting or observing videos).

The manner in which you structure a course – present the flow of topics, or how you name topics – can also represent design. For instance, you may have a course outline that represents all the tasks that a person has to do in order to complete an activity. This would be a task-based content outline – as you saw in the case study on *Entrepreneurship Expedition*. Or you may leverage technology and media in a certain context – as we saw in the *Mathematics Anxiety* case study. Or in some instances, you may weave content around a story to make the learning process appealing – we saw this in the *Financial Inclusion* case study.

To sum up, instructional design may be considered from varied perspectives. If we focus on how the content should be structured, then it is a *content* perspective. If we focus on the tools that should be used to render it in the best possible way, then it is a *technology* or *media* perspective. If we focus on designing and arranging learning events, then it is an *instructional* perspective. We may use a combination of one or more of these, depending upon what we ascertain after analyzing the three variables – the audience, the content, and the learning outcome.

Index

A

ADDIE model
  about 10
  analysis phase 11
  design phase 11
  development phase 12
  evaluation phase 12
  implementation phase 12
  versus Dick and Carey model 14
adult learner
  about 23, 24
  principles 23
American Society for Training and Development (ASTD) 156
analysis
  about 11
  for workplace skills 22
  significance 20-22
Analysis, Design, Development, Implementation, and Evaluation (ADDIE) 10
andragogy
  about 87, 88
  versus pedagogy 88
anecdotal records 155
ARCS model 99, 100
Artificial Intelligence (AI) 133, 163
assessments types
  about 145
  formative assessments 145
  summative assessments 146
asynchronous learning
  about 131
  versus synchronous learning 131
asynchronous online learning
  versus classroom teaching 134, 135

Attention, Relevance, Confidence, and Satisfaction (ARCS) 99

B

behaviorist theory 85
blended learning 132
Bloom's taxonomy
  about 68, 69, 71
  critiquing 71, 72
  example 70
  workaround 72, 73

C

Central Processing Unit (CPU) 113
classroom teaching
  versus asynchronous online learning 134, 135
cognitive load
  about 46, 49, 50
  types 51
cognitive theory 86
Commitment in Relativism phase 34
compact disc read-only memory (CD-ROM) 129
Comprehensive 179
Comprehensive Scaffolding Framework (CSF) 179
concepts
  examples 110
  non-examples 111
Concrete Operational stage 35
constructivist theory 86, 87
content curation 133
content types
  knowledge, presenting 116, 117
content-types framework
  about 108
  concepts 110
  facts 109
  principles 114
  procedures 112
  processes 113
Conventional K-12 curriculum 58
curriculum outline
  about 55
  for higher education 55

D

debt financing
  advantages 177
  disadvantages 177
declarative knowledge
  about 57, 149
  assessing 149
  Fill-in-the-blank 151
  matching questions 151
  multiple choice questions (MCQ) 149, 150
  multi-select questions (MMCQ) 150
  procedural knowledge 153
  subjective questions 152
  versus procedural knowledge 57
demonstration 112
descriptive frameworks
  about 71
  versus prescriptive frameworks 71
design implications 50, 51
design phase
  about 11, 107
  versus development phase 108
design thinking
  versus instructional design 15
Developing A Curriculum (DACUM)
  about 29
  example 30, 31
  scenarios 29
development life cycle (DLC) 25

development phase
  about 12, 107
  versus design phase 108
Dick and Carey model
  about 8-10
  versus ADDIE model 14
direct instruction
  about 89
  applying 94
  principles 90
dual coding 117
Dualism phase 33

E

education analysis
  about 32
  age-related differences 35
  contextual differences 36, 37
  higher education 32, 33
  K-12 34
effectiveness
  versus time/cost 163
effortful retrieval 151
engage component 119
engagement
  versus time/cost 162
entrepreneurship orientation program
  about 171
  background 172
  task-based approach 173-176
equity financing
  advantages 176
  disadvantages 176
evaluation 144, 145
evaluation phase 12
extraneous load 47
  example 48
extrinsic motivation 98

F

financial inclusion program
  about 181
  background 182
  story-based approach 182, 183
flipped classroom 132
Formal Operational stage 36
formative assessments
  about 145
  challenge 147
  designing 146
  feedback 147
  placement 147
  versus summative assessments 146
formative evaluation 12
framework 89
frameworks
  comparing 97

G

Gagne's events of instruction
  about 90, 91
  applying 94
  example 92, 93
germane load 48

H

heutagogy 88, 89

I

implementation phase 12
information communication
    technology (ICT) 6
Information Technology Enabled
    Service (ITES) 76
information technology (IT) 129
instruct component
  about 119
  example 119

instructional design
  constants 3, 4
  decoding 2
  defining 2
  designing 3
  science or art 4, 5
  variables 3, 4
  versus design thinking 15
instructional design certification
  about 177, 178
  background 178, 179
  certification levels 180, 181
  Comprehensive Scaffolding
      Framework (CSF) 179
instructional design models
  about 7, 8, 14
  Dick and Carey model 8
  instructional systems
      design (ISD) model 8
instructional design process 89
instructional design, significance
  about 5
  collaboration, need for 6, 7
  technology evolution 5
instructional material
  overview 13
instructional systems design
      (ISD) model 8
interactivity 100, 101
interleaved practice 167
intrinsic load
  about 46, 47
  example 47
intrinsic motivation 98

J

job aid
  about 122, 123
  checklists 123
  FAQs 123
  flowcharts 123
  if-then tables 123
  infographic 123
  templates 123
job analysis 29, 31

K

Kemp Design model 14
Kirkpatrick model 156
Kolb's Experiential model
  about 95
  applying 96, 97
  stages 96
Kolb's Experiential model, phases
  abstract conceptualization 96
  active experimentation 96
  concrete experience 96
  reflective observation 96

L

learner engagement 100
learner evaluation, types
  formative evaluation 12
learning experience platforms (LXP) 133
learning frameworks
  about 89
  adopting 98
  direct instruction 89
  direct instruction, applying 94
  Gagne's events of instruction 90-92
  Gagne's events
      of instruction, applying 94
  Kolb's Experiential
      model, applying 96, 97
  Merrill's First principles 94
  Merrill's First principles, applying 95
learning management systems
      (LMS) 132, 133
Learning Needs Analysis (LNA) 11

learning outcomes
  concept 65
  frameworks 66
  purpose 66
learning process 128
learning theories
  about 84, 85
  andragogy 87, 88
  behaviorist theory 85
  cognitive theory 86
  constructivist theory 86, 87
  heutagogy 88, 89
  pedagogy 87
long-term memory 43

M

Mager's format
  about 67
  example 67, 68
matching test 151
mathematics anxiety
  about 164
  adaptive approach 165, 166
  background 164, 165
  exercise design 167-170
  personal tutoring 166
memory 42
memory stages 42-44
Merrill's First principles
  about 94
  applying 95
Merrill's First principles, phases
  activation phase 94
  application phase 94
  demonstration phase 94
  integration phase 94
motivation 98
Multiple-Choice Questions (MCQ) 147
multiple-multiple choice questions (MMCQ) 150

Multiplicity phase 33
multi-select questions (MMCQ) 150

O

one-time investment
  versus recurring costs 163
online learning
  asynchronous learning 131
  blended learning 132
  evolution 129, 130
  flipped classroom 132
  synchronous learning 130, 131
  types 130
online learning technology
  about 132
  learning experience platforms (LXP) 133
  learning management systems (LMS) 132, 133
outline design
  about 52
  declarative and procedural knowledge 57, 58
  higher education 55, 56
  K-12 curriculum 58
  vocational skills 56
  workplace learning 52, 53

P

patterning principle 51, 52
patterns 51
pedagogical content knowledge (PCK) 108
pedagogy
  about 87
  versus andragogy 88
pictorial superiority effect (PSE) 117
post-teaching phase 97
Preoperational stage 35
prescriptive frameworks 71

pre-teaching phase 97
principles
   case study 115
   example 114
   scenarios 115
   stories 115, 116
procedural knowledge
   about 57, 152
   anecdotal records 155
   assessing 152, 153
   assessment tools 153
   checklists 154
   rating scales 153
   rubrics 155
   versus declarative knowledge 57
procedures
   example 113
processes
   example 113

R

Rapid Prototyping 14
recurring costs
   versus one-time investment 163
Relativism phase 34
return on investment (ROI) 12
reworked outline 54
rubrics 155

S

Scaffolding 179
schema 48
sector skill council (SSC) 29
self-paced learning 131
Sensorimotor stage 35
sensory memory 43
short-term memory 43
simulation 112
spaced practice 167

storyboard
   about 119
   developing 119
storyboard, components
   engage component 119
   instruct component 119
   teach component 119
storyboard format
   about 120, 121
   audio narration 120
   frame numbers 120
   on-screen text (OST) 120
   visual and programming notes 120
subjective questions 152
subject matter experts (SME) 25
Successive Approximation model
   (SAM) 14
summative assessments
   about 146, 147
   difficulty index 148
   discrimination index 149
   reliability 148
   validity 148
   versus formative assessments 146
summative evaluation 12, 147
synchronous learning
   about 130, 131
   versus asynchronous learning 131

T

teach component 119
teaching phase 97
teaching process 128
terminologies 64
time/cost
   versus effectiveness 163
   versus engagement 162
Training Needs Analysis (TNA) 11
Training ROI
   measuring, challenges 156, 157

V

Value-Expectancy framework 99
varied practice 167
virtual instructor-led teaching (VILT)
  about 128, 136
  breakout rooms, using 137
  online teaching, planning 138, 139
  sessions, collaborating 137
  working 136
visuals
  about 117
  types 118
vocational student 27
vocational training 56

W

Web-based training (WBT) 129
working memory 43-46
workplace analysis
  challenges 25
  example 26
workplace learning 52, 53
workplace training
  evaluation 155
writing learning outcomes
  about 73, 74
  for vocational training 76, 77
  for workplace learning 74
  in higher education 75
  in K-12 77, 78

Made in United States
Troutdale, OR
07/02/2023

10930849R00120